Why **Smart** People Do **Stupid** Things with

MONEY

Overcoming Financial Dysfunction

Bert Whitehead, M.B.A., J.D.

Sterling Publishing Co., Inc.
New York

Library of Congress Cataloging-in-Publication Data

Whitehead, Bert.
  Why smart people do stupid things with money : overcoming financial
dysfunction / Bert Whitehead. — 3rd ed.
      p. cm.
  Includes index.
  Rev ed. of: Facing financial dysfunction / Bert Whitehead. 2nd ed. 2004.
  ISBN-13: 978-1-4027-4734-2
  ISBN-10: 1-4027-4734-9
1. Finance, Personal. I. Whitehead, Bert. Facing financial dysfunction. II.
Title.

HG179.W5243 2007
332.024—dc22

2006038574

1 2 3 4 5 6 7 8 9 10

Published by Sterling Publishing Co., Inc.
387 Park Avenue South, New York, NY 10016
©2007 by Bert Whitehead
Distributed in Canada by Sterling Publishing
c/o Canadian Manda Group, 165 Dufferin Street,
Toronto, Ontario, Canada M6K 3H6
Distributed in the United Kingdom by GMC Distribution Services,
Castle Place, 166 High Street, Lewes, East Sussex, England BN7 1XU
Distributed in Australia by Capricorn Link (Australia) Pty. Ltd.
P.O. Box 704, Windsor, NSW 2756, Australia

Manufactured in the United States of America
All rights reserved

Sterling ISBN-13: 978-1-4027-4734-2
          ISBN-10: 1-4027-4734-9

For information about custom editions, special sales, premium, and
corporate purchases, please contact Sterling Special Sales
Department at 800-805-5489 or specialsales@sterlingpub.com.

Parts of this book originally appeared in *Facing Financial Dysfunction: Why Smart People Do
Stupid Things with Money!* (2nd edition, 1994, Infinity Publishing.com) by Bert Whitehead.
Some of the material in this book appeared previously in *Overcoming Financial Dysfunction:
How to Make Smarter Decisions About Money* (a companion workbook to Facing Financial
Dysfunction), copyright ©2005 by Bert Whitehead, Infinity Publishing.com, West
Conshohocken, Pennsylvania; written by Bert Whitehead and Kenneth F. Robinson; this
material appears by permission of Ken Robinson. This edition contains substantial updates to
the previous edition and significantly more explanatory material.

To the Cambridge Family: The advisors and staff of Cambridge Connection, Inc.; the Cambridge Advisors I have trained who have taken this message and validated it all over the United States; the hundreds of my Cambridge clients, past and present, I personally have worked with; and finally, to the thousands of Cambridge clients served today by members of the Cambridge Alliance of Fee-Only Personal Financial Advisors across the country. Through them I have learned what is in this book.

Acknowledgments

My mission is to make fee-only personal financial planning accessible to real people. This book represents a big milestone on the way toward that goal. It is the story of a new age in financial planning that is still in the early adopter stage.

To go forward with ideas that challenge the entrenched establishment takes more than one person. Left to my own devices, this book would never have been written. Without the people who believed in these ideals, I would have abandoned the mission or just gone into my little space in the world. But with their support, I found the courage to keep at it. This book is the story of what I have learned from the people to whom I've dedicated it.

Writing this book has been both torturous and exhilarating. I want to acknowledge the prime mover in the project, my friend Josh Pokempner. He nagged me nonstop to share my ideas. Gail Whitty, my very first client over 35 years ago, must have been in cahoots with him. A stalwart believer in fee-only planning, she has supported and encouraged me continually over the years. Cathy Stegmaier, who has worked with me for over ten years, actually did a lot of the work on the original (preview) edition. Anne Lesser, a professional writer and Cambridge client, single-handedly enabled me to get the earlier editions to the publisher. I am especially grateful to Al Hoefer, my technical editor. After he read the preview edition, he applied his high-level skills to the concepts; his wisdom, expertise, and common sense show up in the revised graphics he provided for this edition. And, evaluating his own financial plan, he has since become a client.

I am grateful to my staff for their unique abilities that help keep me on track. In particular, Jason Moore, my senior associate, assisted in editing the graphs and charts that were developed by staff members. Sana Shamsi and Anita Rajpal have both assisted me with research and with technical advice.

Ken Robinson, who coauthored a companion workbook, *Overcoming Financial Dysfunction,* with me, has graciously given permission to use material from that workbook in this edition.

My guru, Dan Sullivan, has put up with me as his maverick for more than ten years in the Strategic Coach Program. By putting his entrepreneurial concepts into action in my life, I have transformed the way I work. Writing this book was one of the goals I set in my first session with him years ago. I used Dan's project planning tool, the Strategic Circle, to develop this project from just a concept through to completion.

Many other clients and Cambridge Advisors have cheered me along the way. Kathleen Rehl, Bob Brock, Linda Laraia, Robert Walsh, Neil Powell, Harry Cohen, Pam Landy, Marta McKenna, and many others reviewed the early drafts and made constructive suggestions. A special thank-you to my son, Tiger Whitehead, who brought his dad into the computer age and evaluated the readability of the text.

Most of all, I am indebted to Carol Johnson, my life partner, for bringing this book home. She spent countless hours copyediting. She too is a true believer in my mission and an enthusiastic supporter of Cambridge. Many people believe in this story. I hope it will be recognized not only as a seminal work in our profession but also as a practical handbook for my readers.

Contents

Foreword

Because Bert Whitehead has been my financial advisor since the 1980s, I have been able to follow the development of his concepts as presented in this book. He is one of the pioneers of fee-only personal financial planning and dedicated to elevating that vocation to the level of a profession.

I didn't consider myself financially dysfunctional before I met Bert, but I was often confused by competing offers from various stockbrokers and money managers to help me. Bert's Financial Life Cycle idea made sense to me and enabled me to understand why my situation required the strategies he proposed. Moreover, his Functional Asset Allocation ("the pyramid") allowed me to see my whole portfolio, including my real estate holdings, as an interrelated wealth base rather than as isolated assets.

In our meetings, Bert often asked me about the growing problems of the medical profession and the impact of the integrative medicine movement, which has been my life's work. He was quick to see the parallels in our two professions. Integrative medicine's approach has made the consumer aware there is more to medicine than what conventional doctors recommend and what pharmaceutical companies and insurance companies provide.

Consumer demand for something more is forcing the medical profession to change. Already a number of leading medical schools throughout the country are beginning to train physicians in this new system. In the same way, the ideas in this book have resonated with thousands of clients throughout the country and are beginning to impact the profession of financial planning.

Over the past 15 years, I have been through major life changes, both personal and professional. Having a fee-only advisor with an integrative approach, who helps me with all aspects of my financial life, has been most reassuring. I am certain it will soon become the standard. It seems obvious that financial advisors are hired by clients to be their agents; advisors should not be in the position of having to sell advice an employer dictates.

This book offers the vision for this new relationship between advisors and clients—a fee-only approach. There is no agenda to promote any particular financial product. Bert tells me that other qualified advisors have validated the system. I can say that the use of these concepts has made the financial world more comprehensible to me and has made a positive difference in my life.

—Andrew Weil, M.D.

Introduction

I decided to write this book to showcase key concepts of behavioral finance that are revolutionizing financial planning. These new concepts represent a break from the traditional left-brain approach to financial planning that favors economic and mathematical analysis to solve financial issues. This new view of financial planning recognizes that people's reactions are not purely rational when it comes to money. This paradigm reflects the values of an emerging profession of true fee-only personal advisors.

The practitioners of this new profession are demonstrating that the general public wants more from the financial industry than salespeople and asset gatherers who masquerade as financial planners even though they do not establish a fiduciary relationship with clients. While fiduciaries are required to put the client's interests ahead of their own, sales reps are free to recommend whatever investment pays them the highest commissions. I am not shy in this book about bashing the financial industry at large

> **I am not shy in this book about bashing the financial industry at large for foisting pitches on middle income people.**

for foisting sales pitches on middle-income people. I would like to say at the outset, however, that the financial industry, including the stockbrokers, insurance companies, mutual fund companies, and the like—in spite of their shortcomings—have made an invaluable contribution to our country and our way of life.

Over the past 50 years in particular, the financial industry has marshaled the savings of millions of people to fuel the expansion of the U.S. economy and produce unparalleled levels of employment in a changed world. The skills required in today's economy are vastly different from those that were needed in the 1950s. The capital generated through our financial institutions has made the transformation of our society possible. We have been able to upgrade the technology available to small businesses and individuals as well as corporate giants. We have completely retrained our labor force to keep people working and help companies reach unprecedented levels of productivity. This transformation is no small feat; it has been driven by efficient capital formation for which the financial industry can justly take credit.

> "Over the past 50 years . . . the financial industry has marshaled the savings of millions of people to fuel the expansion of the U.S. economy . . . ."

The concept of pooling the investments of small investors using mutual funds has enabled the financial industry to spread the risk of this new age of capital adventure we have embarked on. At the same time, it has given ordinary Americans, most of whom are small investors, an opportunity to enjoy a stake in our economic progress and a share of the profits it has created.

The adoption of Social Security marked the beginning of the era of pooling the assets of small investors. The adoption of defined-benefit pensions by many companies followed, accelerated by the power of labor unions. The Second World War sparked a huge interest in savings bonds (called war bonds then) as a patriotic way for Americans to invest in their country.

In the 1950s, life insurance companies started vigorously marketing various types of permanent insurance. These policies provided tax advantages and enabled people to protect themselves and accumulate money at the same time. Mutual funds began to expand their offerings, which gave small investors the advantages of diversification.

Beginning in the 1970s, when inflation was rampant and the stock market slumped for a period of 15 years, small investors started to realize that not all the investments they had been sold were appropriate for their situation. The financial industry continued to bring out increasingly complex products, enabling companies to attach high marketing costs.

Real estate limited partnerships became the fad, and then came junk bonds and collateralized mortgage obligations. These very complex vehicles, I am sure, were not even understood completely by the investment advisors who were selling them. This ignorance was (and still is) in large part due to the lack of credentials and appropriate training and education required of financial advisors.

In the 1980s, the consumer movement and the media began examining conflicts of interest in the financial industry. Technically, the Securities and Exchange Commission (SEC) required sales commissions to be disclosed. In practice, these commissions were buried in small print in unreadable prospectuses. Even monthly statements for customers obfuscated the commissions investors were paying, by listing only the number of shares they held and the price per share. The total value was not shown because it would have been too easy to spot how much commission was charged, particularly right after the sale. Moreover, disclosure has never been required of insurance companies, which are regulated by individual states. Even today, insurance companies do not disclose the unconscionable commissions that motivate their agents to push products.

In the early 1990s, a few independent but notable journalists, such as Jane Bryant Quinn, Bob Veres, and consumer writers for the *Wall Street Journal,* began to highlight the abuses in the financial industry. Their disclosures prompted some changes by the industry, but these were mostly window dressing. Instead of charging commissions upfront (i.e., front-end loads), the industry adopted the practice of using so-called surrender charges. Supposedly, no commission was charged if the investment was held for 5 years. If it was cashed in during the first year, a commission of about 5% would be deducted as a surrender charge. This was reduced 1% a year, so after 5 years it looked as if there was no commission being charged at all.

In fact, a new annual sales charge of about 1%, called a 12b-1 load, was assessed annually on the total value of these investments, designated B shares. Clearly, this charge offset the declining surrender charge: salespeople were paid exactly the same commission, but this smoke-and-mirrors tactic enabled them to disingenuously exclaim, "No front-end loads!"

Insurance companies also used this device, even more aggressively, in teaching their agents (i.e., salespeople) to sell annuities. Annuities are basically investments wrapped in a life insurance policy; they generally have very high expenses and pay outrageous commissions. Legitimate uses for annuities are very few, and include extreme asset protection schemes. Objective financial experts are virtually in unanimous agreement that annuities don't make sense as investments. In fact, they are mostly marketed to the most vulnerable segments of our population: older people for safety and tax shelters, and naive young investors for IRAs.

In reality, older people are usually in a 25% tax bracket or lower and don't need a tax shelter. For the annuity owner, there is no more safety in a mutual fund wrapped in an annuity than one held outside (neither one is federally guaranteed). Plus, at death, the beneficiaries are saddled with paying taxes on earnings generated within the annuity at their ordinary tax rates, which can be as high as 45%, depending on a beneficiary's tax bracket and state of residence. By contrast, if the beneficiaries inherited the mutual funds outside the annuity, they would receive a tax-free step-up in basis—in other words, there would be no tax triggered upon the death of the owner. They would receive the full amount with no ordinary or capital gains tax due. IRAs are themselves tax deferred, so there is absolutely no reason to put them in an annuity.

The annuity has a small life insurance policy, which only pays out if the investment has dropped below the original cost at the time of death. The premium paid for that paltry protection is outrageous. The only positive feature of this financial instrument is the ability to transfer funds from one mutual fund to another within the annuity without triggering taxes. Because doing this can also be accomplished within IRAs, it is absurd to think that this feature is worth the price of having the profits eventually taxed as ordinary income to the heirs. Even outside an IRA, it is advantageous to have an owner pay taxes on profits at the capital gains rate, which, when applicable, is generally about half the regular ordinary tax rate. This is preferable to unintentionally pushing beneficiaries into higher tax brackets when they are forced to declare all of the earnings as ordinary income at the owner's death.

> **As abuses in the financial industry have come to light . . . the industry has been forced to mature considerably.**

The only reason annuities are sold is because they pay about 50% more commission than regular mutual funds. These are the dirty little secrets of our industry, which only started to be exposed on a wide scale at the consumer level in the late 1980s. Since then, it has begun dawning on the investing public that their stockbroker, insurance agent, or financial planner may not have their best interests in mind.

The financial industry has gone through many changes as a result of this evolution. The CFP designation (for Certified Financial Planner) has become the accepted standard for advisors. The CFP Board of Standards has tightened its requirements, particularly over the past ten years; however, CFPs are not yet required to adopt a fiduciary standard in dealings with their clients. The National Association of Personal Financial Advisors (NAPFA) was born in the 1980s to promote fee-only financial planning. Its members take a fiduciary oath for the benefit of their clients.

As abuses in the financial industry have come to light and mushroomed because of a new awareness of inherent conflicts of interest, the industry has been forced to mature considerably. This glacial change has shifted stockbrokers and insurance salespeople from earning commissions to monitoring clients' investment assets for a percentage of assets under management. As we discuss in Appendix A ("Where to Find a True Fee-Only Personal Financial Advisor"), this approach is still rife with conflicts, but it is definitely a step forward from commission-based compensation.

To its credit, the industry is increasingly aware that the financial advisor's position requires a professional, broad-scale, multidisciplinary approach to clients' financial concerns. Dalbar surveys, used extensively in our industry, clearly point out that clients prefer an unbiased advisor who will educate them personally and show them how to integrate their financial situation to cut their taxes and give them peace of mind. The most forward-thinking fee-only financial advisors have expanded their practices to emphasize financial coaching and encompass life planning.

> **The concepts I explain in this book are at the heart of this new frontier of financial planning.**

The concepts I explain in this book are at the heart of this new frontier of financial planning. These ideas are not ivory tower notions. I have developed them experientially over the past 35 years in practice, watching what clients did in real life and analyzing which approaches were successful. Thus these financial strategies are based on more than a thousand real-life client experiences over a long period of time.

The idea of graphically illustrating the Money Personality Matrix, the Cambridge Financial Life Cycle, and the Functional Asset Allocation Pyramid was developed over many years of trial and error. I find these visual aids exceptionally effective in explaining these complex concepts to my clients.

Most important from a professional point of view, other practitioners have validated these concepts. Over the past 20 years, I have trained more than 200 qualified fee-only personal financial advisors in the use of these theories. Many members of the Alliance of Cambridge Advisors have made suggestions as well. Often, these ideas, based on their own experiences with clients, were adapted and incorporated into these concepts. They, in turn, have used these approaches with their own clients, totaling well over 10,000 at this printing.

To my knowledge, this is the first time a comprehensive theory of financial planning for middle-income people has been developed and validated by qualified practitioners and enthusiastically received by clients. To me this is what a profession is all about: the development of approaches by practitioners rather than by the financial industry itself, which has something to sell. Until now, financial planning formats were developed primarily to sell financial products.

This book is designed to offer you, the consumer, a different perspective, reflecting the history of our economic system and the changes taking place right now. Based on my 36 years as a professional in this field (as of this writing in 2007), it is apparent to me that the public is more dissatisfied with the financial guidance available than ever before. I hope it will help you understand that the process must start with you. You can then leverage the insights you discover about yourself, using these time-tested, revolutionary new approaches to achieve financial freedom.

Financial Freedom

> People who don't respect money don't have any.
>
> —J. PAUL GETTY

The industrial world we live in today has brought us many benefits. However, it has also brought us some now-familiar problems, including the dysfunctions we see in our physical bodies and in our families.

In the same way, our modern society has made it more difficult for us to keep operating financially. Most people avoid dealing with their finances because they feel baffled, dissatisfied, and distrustful. Our financial affairs are just too complicated and too time-demanding for us to stay on top of them properly. We know we should put in a few hours a week to examine whether we are saving enough each month and investing as efficiently and wisely as we can. At the same time, we are expected to navigate a career, manage a household, guide the kids, and keep up with mortgage payments. We also want to eat better and get more exercise. We want to be free from our financial worries—free to live our lives without the nagging feeling that we are stuck. But how do we do it?

HOW WE HELP

For over 35 years, I have worked as a fee-only personal financial advisor assisting middle-income families. I have had the privilege to train more than two hundred other financial advisors across the country. In our offices, my professional colleagues and I look after the financial affairs of our clients, many of whom just do not have the time to do it. We help them become fiscally free—free from dysfunctional thinking and behaviors and, eventually, free from the need to work.

> **Most people avoid dealing with their finances because they feel baffled, dissatisfied, and distrustful.**

I advise my clients on decisions that nonfinancial people have difficulty figuring out. Should they buy or lease a car, or what is the best way for them to fund a child's education? We also provide professional expertise in the areas that have become too complex for individuals to handle themselves, such as preparing personal income tax returns or balancing investment portfolios.

We have two tremendous advantages over the typical advisors who work for insurance companies or stock brokerages: (1) We are pure fee-only fiduciary advisors, and (2) we take a holistic approach to family finances. Let me explain these key concepts.

First, pure fee-only personal financial advisors do not receive commissions or any compensation from third parties (generally known as kickbacks). We work in a fiduciary relationship with our clients and consider ourselves their agents: Clients hire us to find the best solution for them. Most so-called financial advisors have a hidden agenda—to sell whatever their employer sells—so they harbor a conflict of interest. Even investment advisors who charge a percentage of assets under management cannot give unbiased advice about rolling over your 401(k) or paying off the mortgage on your home because these transactions would impact their compensation.

Second, as pure fee-only personal financial advisors we are committed to integrating all aspects of our clients' finances. Most people get frustrated because they are going one place for tax assistance, another for investment advice, somewhere else for insurance coverage, and yet another place for estate planning. Usually clients don't even understand most of the gobbledygook used in the financial world, and the people they are relying on for advice aren't talking to one another. (If you are interested in hiring a pure fee-only personal financial advisor, see Appendix A.)

The greatest feature of the holistic financial advising approach is that it's free from conflicts of interest. In rare cases where conflicts do arise, they are disclosed to clients; if there is a significant amount at stake, a fiduciary advisor may be required to recuse herself. This method helps you develop your financial fitness, which follows a course that is the reverse of the usual course of a person's physical functioning. Instead of the slow degeneration that comes with age, your financial life can grow bigger, stronger, and more fit every year of your life. We encourage people to set goals for themselves and not be too conservative about them. Most of our clients have discovered that they can accomplish pretty much whatever they want as long as personal financial advisors are coaching them to make sure the details are in place.

As pure fee-only advisors, we only charge for the services we render. We don't try to sell you anything on commission. Yes, there is a market for people who sell products on commission. However, for my financial advice, I'd much rather go where I know it's not geared to the interest of the salesperson and a large and distant corporation. Our advice is more objective, and we work hard at keeping our fees low and entirely visible.

I started in this business in 1971. As you can imagine, I've seen a lot of changes in the financial fitness of our communities. When I started my practice, people would come to me for advice about what deductions the tax code would allow. They would ask for an unbiased opinion on whether they should buy the life insurance policy an agent was recommending as a total financial panacea. Often, the alternative was a stockbroker's recommendation to buy a mutual fund that had managed to own the right stocks one year and post an outrageous return. The insurance agent showed impressive spreadsheets to prove that an investor would be a millionaire in fifty-two years; the broker touted the mutual fund as an almost sure bet to double an investment every year. Which alternative should they choose?

Those were the good old days in financial advising. A lot of salespeople were pretending to be in my business, but back then they were quite clumsy about disguising their agendas and weaknesses. We could show our clients which investments served their personal and financial goals and which ones only served the interests of the people selling them. Meanwhile, their employer took care of their retirement income needs with pensions that lasted for the lifetimes of the client and spouse. So most of our work went into making sure they got into the habit of putting some of their income into investments every year and building a secure financial base so they could spend some time enjoying life, family, relationships, and all the other important things too often ignored in a busy lifestyle.

Today, it isn't so easy for most people. The most significant shift is that now most people cannot rely on employer-supplied "defined-benefit" pensions to ensure a comfortable retirement. In addition, it seems that today people have a lot more responsibilities, which means they have less time and attention to devote to developing their financial competence.

People come to me with the weight of the world on their shoulders. They want to support their children into maturity, even though they themselves were told at a certain age to fend for themselves and, after some fumbling around, they discovered that they could. They also want to offer at least partial support to their aging parents, who retired on a fixed income and now, for the first time in many years, are feeling stressed about their own financial situation.

FINANCIAL COMPLICATIONS

Meanwhile, our society has created some really nasty complications in the financial world. Taxes have gotten monumentally more complex over the last 35 years, to the point where even we professionals complain about all the work we have to put in to stay on top of them. In the financial advising business, we think that congressional tinkering with the tax laws every year makes many people feel dysfunctional. All this misery could be entirely prevented if we would just get the tax code down on a couple of pages in plain English.

Many people find themselves dysfunctional when it comes to investing, a very simple activity that almost everybody, for some mysterious reason, gets wrong. We financial professionals shake our heads when we see magazine covers screaming "The Ten Funds to Buy Now!" and for some reason the same 10 mutual funds are recommended to every reader, no matter what their age, goals, or financial situation. You'll read articles in which writers claim to have some kind of clairvoyance about the future, and nobody ever accuses them of financial malpractice. Because such articles are printed in glossy magazines, our clients take them seriously. Unless we help them understand the possible exceptions to the broad generalizations they have read, they will follow this enormous herd whose only investment creed seems to be to buy high, sell low, and take as much risk as possible along the way.

> **We are entering a "YOYO" economy: You're on your own!**

As fee-only fiduciary advisors, we do what we can with our own clients around the country, but we're frustrated that we're not redirecting the larger herd of people moving blindly in the wrong direction. Everybody in the herd is too busy to give these matters much thought or attention. If people find their way to us, we help them, but there is a scarcity of credentialed, ethical, professional fee-only financial advisors. (If you are interested, or know someone who is interested, in becoming qualified as a fee-only financial advisor, refer to Appendix B.)

Meanwhile, millions more have no advisor at all or at best a salesperson masquerading as a financial advisor. These people never realize that their financial lives are suffering because they took the advice they saw in the latest issue of *Money* magazine or from the latest talking head on CNBC.

New investment alternatives require new tactics. For example, stock options have become increasingly available to lower-level employees, especially in newer start-up technology companies.

These options have a number of variations, such as "nonqualified stock options," "incentive stock options," and so on. Many have cockeyed rules attached to them, which are all wrong for long-term investing. People can actually receive stock options and do with them what they were intended for, which is to buy stock in their employer's company. However, as soon as the options are exercised, they are taxed on the "bargain element," which is the difference between their option price and the current market price. This amount can be most of the value of the stock, and is taxable as wages and included in the employee's W-2. If the stock then nosedives (which is not uncommon with volatile stocks), these investors (that is, the employees) may lose as much as 90% of their investment. Since the loss on the investment is a "capital loss," it doesn't offset the bargain element included in their wages. As a result they come away with a huge tax bill to the IRS. Can you imagine that? It's not a pretty sight.

There is more, of course. The rules on Roth IRAs and charitable giving are more complicated than the average person has the patience to learn. The professionals at all our offices make sure people know enough to make smart choices, and we check that the paperwork gets filled out properly for federal, state, or local agencies. Who has the time to do this themselves anymore—and have a life at the same time?

People today are changing jobs more frequently, retiring earlier, and living longer—and they expect to have more and do more at every stage of their lives than the people we were seeing just a few years ago. Almost none of our younger clients can expect to receive an employer-paid pension, and their confidence in having Social Security and Medicare take care of them into old age is not high. We are entering a "YOYO" economy: "You're on your own!" The next generation of retirees have to do it all themselves, and there usually isn't a lot of time.

Much has changed in 35 years, but the bottom line has remained the same. The people who asked us to look after their financial development in 1972 asked the same important questions about their lives that the people who visit us ask today. How am I really doing? As well I could

> **The good news is that these problems can all be solved. The much better news is that most of them can be prevented.**

be? Will I have enough to retire? Will my children be able to attend the college of their choice? Will we ever be able to stop fighting about money? Why do I feel so stuck?

THE GOOD NEWS

These questions, along with the other issues I have discussed, represent today's most common financial problems. The good news is that these problems can all be solved. The much better news is that most of them can be prevented. It is not hard to meet your financial goals if you know how to go about it and are willing to make at least a minimum commitment to the process. In fact, many people, once they get the hang of it, have some fun along the way and eventually become much more than fiscally fit. They also achieve peace of mind.

In our professional practice, we see every kind of financial dysfunction. We think to ourselves, "If only these people could have a simple guide to their finances written in layperson's language." I wrote this book in the same style that I talk to my clients. Occasionally, for emphasis, I do jump from the third person to the second, and then to the first to weave in my personal experiences.

Right-brained people will intuitively understand and appreciate the first six chapters of the book, which deal with behavioral finance issues like the Money Personality Matrix and the Financial Life Cycle. It may be more difficult for them to wade through the technical details of Functional Asset Allocation, which will appeal to their left-brained counterparts. I have woven in enough numbers in the first six chapters to appeal to the left-brainers, and in the last three chapters I have integrated some great stories that I hope will keep the attention of you right-brainers.

So this book is for you, whoever you are and whatever your state of financial freedom may be right now. It is not a professional treatise on the subject but rather a common-sense guide that will give you the information you need to achieve and maintain financial freedom.

What Is Financial Dysfunction?

> Investment must be rational. If you can't understand it, don't do it.
> —WARREN BUFFETT

My profession has a few basic principles that describe the various ways people can lose their financial freedom. I call them financial dysfunctions. They're a little like not eating right and not getting enough exercise—except I think everybody knows they should eat right and exercise. In my world, people have ideas about financial behavior that are just plain wrong. I define financial dysfunctions as financial choices and strategies that people believe are effective but that actually impede their financial progress.

When I was deciding on a title and subtitle for this book, a few people thought the term *financial dysfunction* was too negative. Many more, however, instantly recognized its significance and, more importantly, saw that it applied to their own lives.

Financial dysfunction leads to intense stress, which shows up in family relationships as anger and quarreling. Often, financial stress disrupts sleep patterns, resulting in either insomnia or being tired all the time. At its worst, financial issues precipitate acute depression or at least a chronic dissatisfaction with life in general, which I think is one of the worst symptoms a person could experience. I have named this syndrome *deprivation anxiety*. It shows up when people literally can't sleep because of worries about finances, when couples bicker about who is spending too much, or when the partner in charge of the finances keeps the purse strings tight, always insisting that "We don't have enough money for that!"

Sometimes the pain gets so bad that people are driven to come into one of our offices, even though they have only a vague idea of what we do and how it relates to their financial health. They feel confused about all the paperwork and uncertain about what it will take to meet all their financial obligations. They feel guilty that they haven't put more time into their financial development, and a surprising number of them realize that there is no quick fix.

When they see that I understand their dissatisfaction and have worked with many other people with the same problems, they smile with relief. Of course, I tell them that their situation is not hopeless, and then I help them realize that their financial problems are caused, in most cases, by factors they can control. For example, money is a taboo subject in many, if not most, families. People never talk around the dinner table about money the way they talk about sports. Many grow up to be really good at handicapping the chances of their favorite football or baseball team, but not so good at figuring out which deductions they are or are not entitled to under Code Section 408(a) governing Roth IRAs. Most Americans aren't even sure if it is best to pay off their mortgage or not and don't know how to diversify their portfolio.

Another issue underlying financial dysfunction is the thousands of people who advertise themselves as trusted advisors but are really nothing more than salespeople. This isn't to say that salespeople can't behave honorably, although it is suspicious when a client is sold an inappropriate investment that carries the highest rate of commission. We see a lot of people in our offices who have been given bad advice, and they didn't have any way to recognize it until their financial distress was painfully apparent.

Still another factor contributing to financial dysfunction is the media. Many well-meaning people host or participate in the various financial programs that run all day and all night on cable TV. Their overall effect on people's financial competence and success, I can tell you from experience, is not positive. You happen to tune into one of the programs and see a mutual fund manager predicting the direction of interest rates and the bottom of the market. There is generous prompting from the host of the program, who makes sure to ask for a few hot stock tips after they break for a commercial.

In addition, of course, the commercial itself is for an online brokerage company that will give you access to the markets for day trading at discounted commissions. To encourage gambling in stocks is worse than spreading a disease; it is promoting an activity as addictive as a lethal drug that destroys people's lives. And it seems to me that even the hosts of these programs don't realize they work hand in glove with the companies that earn trading commissions every time somebody acts on those hot tips that are delivered reliably on the half-hour. No wonder people have trouble staying on top of their financial lives!

I like our clients to recognize the environmental factors that led to their declining financial situations. In this way they can see that their financial dysfunctions are understandable and even predictable—and, most importantly, not their fault. While they are getting on top of things, we try to identify the specific financial dysfunction that relates to each separate issue and help them avoid it in the future. Clients may not be responsible for their prior dysfunctional patterns, but they *are* responsible for dealing with them once they become aware of how to do that.

SPRINGBOARDS OF FINANCIAL DYSFUNCTION

Let's examine some of the springboards of financial dysfunction, and then explore in more detail how this dysfunction manifests itself in people's financial and personal lives.

#1: Lack of Awareness of Your Financial Personality

People are not aware of their own financial personalities or the common dysfunctions to which they are prone. If you are not making the financial progress you want to be making, the first place to look is at yourself. By getting to know yourself, as well as the inappropriate behavior you might be predisposed to display, you take a big step toward changing your financial life. We help you assess your own financial personality in Chapter 3 and then acquaint you with seven common symptoms of financial dysfunction in Chapter 4.

> If you are not making the financial progress you want to be making, the first place to look is at yourself.

#2: Relying on Factors Outside Your Control

People tend to believe that exogenous factors (those factors that are *externally* generated, such as interest rates or the price of oil) are more important than endogenous factors (factors that are *internally* generated in their lives, such as how much they earn, how much debt they are carrying, and how they handle credit). This is a fancy way of saying they really control their own financial destiny—even though that seems to be impossible, with all the distractions going on around us and the day's complicated market activities summarized in glorious detail on the hour. Once people understand that they are in control, that what they do will have much more of a bearing on their future than all the rest of the things going on outside, they start to make progress toward financial freedom in a hurry.

For example, in 2002 a client called me who was very agitated about the possibility of war in the Mideast, asking whether he should stop investing in the stock market. My reply was, "Why? Are you getting drafted?" World events that make the news (war is an exogenous factor) seldom have an impact on our financial situation, unless somehow our lives are directly affected by their repercussions (getting drafted is an endogenous factor).

Without this understanding, people can never take command of their own lives and circumstances. The exogenous paradigm, which assumes that our finances depend on issues outside of us, is deadly. The ramifications of our environment, the impact of the media, the sales tactics of many so-called financial advisors, and the inappropriate approaches applied to family financial issues all perpetuate this paradigm. These issues are discussed in Chapter 5, and in Chapter 6, we talk about how to shift to an endogenous paradigm, one that proceeds from your own situation.

#3: Inability to Benchmark Progress

Most people have no idea if they are on target financially (i.e., if they are progressing financially at an adequate rate). Because money is a taboo topic, they are never sure if their neighbors are really better off than they are or where they should be financially at a given age. Many people who walk into our offices have never even taken the time to figure out what they want out of life. What could be more important for them? How do you know you're making progress if you don't have a clear idea of where you want to go? How do you know you're in good enough financial shape to send your children to college or to retire eventually?

Without this understanding, people are never sure how much is enough or even if they are on the right track. In Chapter 7 we introduce the Financial Life Cycle, which for the first time enables people to benchmark themselves financially. You will see exactly where you stand financially and where you should be at your age. Most important, I explain in detail the strategies you must use to progress from stage to stage.

#4: Using Tools and Strategies Designed for Other People's Needs

Almost everything you might read about investing for the future was developed for an audience that is not you. Most investment theories we use today were developed by academics to improve the efficient monitoring of huge pension-fund portfolios.

Investment houses employ underqualified people to use these inappropriate concepts to advise families; the main objective is promoting their own financial products. I am sorry to tell you this, but surprisingly little thinking has been done about the financial problems of people who lead the familiar life you see around you. Where do you see an investment plan that takes into account the fact that your mortgage payments are crushing for the first couple of years and seem almost incidental ten or fifteen years later?

> **Almost everything you read about investing for the future was developed for an audience that is not you.**

Until you realize that most of the financial information you read is either wrong or doesn't apply to you, it is impossible to stay on course. You will constantly experience more than your share of financial problems, leading to that feeling of chronic dissatisfaction and deprivation anxiety I mentioned earlier. In Chapter 8, we discuss a revolutionary new approach to structuring and allocating a family's assets and investments. Functional Asset Allocation has been used with tens of thousands of clients and by hundreds of fee-only advisors. It is a simple but extremely efficient model to understand and guide a family's finances.

Most important, you don't need to accept financial dysfunction in your life. In nearly all the cases we see, you can begin by redirecting your focus and figuring out where you currently stand financially. Then you can lay out some ideas about how you want to measure your progress, get somebody to coach you, and take care of the paperwork. You will rapidly see changes in your situation and experience the security and confidence that comes with being financially functional.

Unfortunately, for some this is not easy. There is so much quackery in our financial environment that people are brainwashed with the equivalent of old wives' tales and home-brewed remedies. These elixirs are always much more complicated and expensive than the basic things we should be doing in our financial lives. Chapter 9 discusses these issues.

TIME TO CHANGE

Start by examining your own personality and changing your belief systems. Make a decision to shift to an endogenous paradigm, one based on your own situation. Benchmark your progress to see where you are and where you should be. Develop strategies to get where you want to go, and adopt a functional approach to implementing your strategy. Then, either change your behavior on your own or have a financial professional keep track and coach you gently to do what you can't make yourself do on your own. Financial professionals will also identify areas where you may need in-depth financial counseling in a series of frequent face-to-face meetings. When outside professional assistance is called for, these professionals will be able to suggest resources. Appendix A provides information on how to evaluate and access these resources.

> **Start by examining your own personality and changing your belief systems.**

Do these things and nothing more! The odds are good that you will, sooner rather than later, begin to achieve both freedom from worry and sound financial fitness.

Your Financial Personality

> He who is frugal is the richest of men, and the miser is the poorest.
>
> ———NICOLAS CHAMFORT

People typically walk into our offices with three symptoms: They are baffled, dissatisfied, and distrustful.

- They're baffled because with so many choices in their everyday lives, it is often hard to identify the right one.
- They're *dissatisfied* because they can't figure out a way to measure their progress as the years slip by faster and faster. They aren't sure how they are really doing compared to others or in relation to their own goals.
- And they're *distrustful* because they know that many people who pose as financial advisors are actually trying to sell them something.

I start by helping them discover who they are and how their money personality can aggravate their financial situation. Different people have different financial capabilities.

KNOW THYSELF

To understand your own financial personality, let's look at where you would fit on what I call the Money Personality Matrix, which can help you define your money personality. The first dimension of the matrix is a measure of risk acceptance or risk aversion (see Figure 3.1). It is well documented in the literature of my profession (and I have seen proof with my own eyes in over 30 years of practice) that two key emotions motivate us financially: fear and greed.

Traditional financial jargon refers to those motivated by fear as *low risk* and those motivated by greed as *high risk*. Personally, I believe greed is a word loaded with negative connotations, but let's suspend that thought for a minute. Think of people at the upper end of the greed/fear scale as those who feel that it is important to accumulate

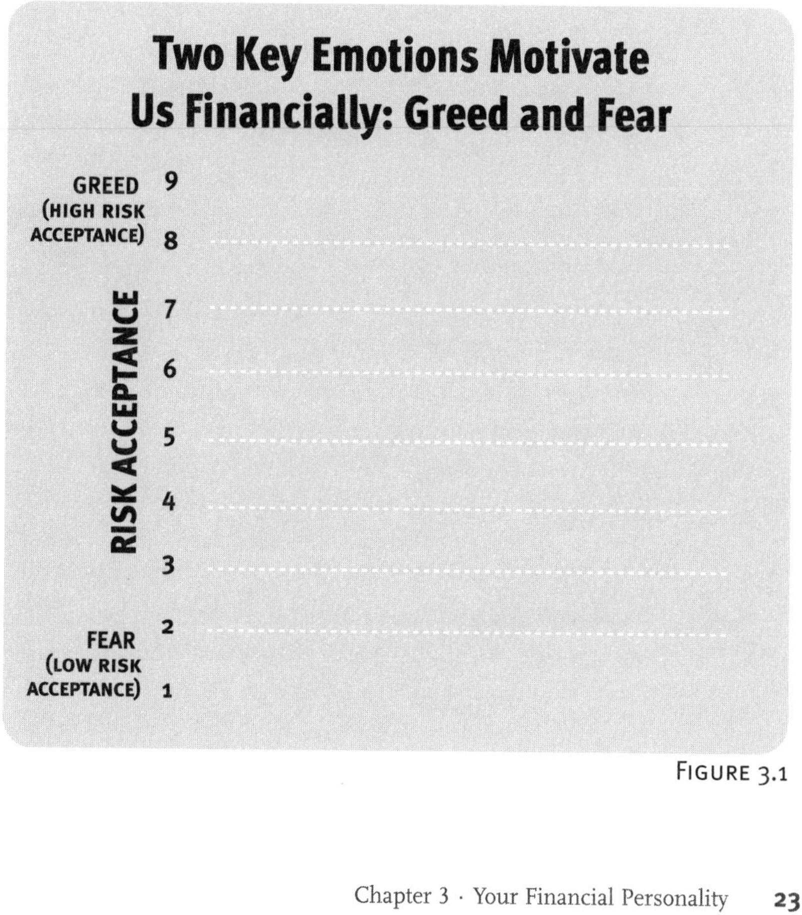

Two Key Emotions Motivate Us Financially: Greed and Fear

GREED (HIGH RISK ACCEPTANCE) 9
8

RISK ACCEPTANCE 7
6
5
4
3

FEAR (LOW RISK ACCEPTANCE) 2
1

FIGURE 3.1

financial assets. People on the lower end of the scale, toward the fear end, are driven not to lose the money they have earned. Take the quiz in Exercise 3.1, "Score Your Risk Acceptance," and estimate on the vertical scale where you would rank on the spectrum of fear and greed.

People also seem to come into this world with their own unique *spending propensity*. This is another of my profession's fancy phrases; it means some people tend to be savers, those who actually enjoy squeezing money out of their budgets. Others tend to be spenders; they like to spend every penny they get. You might think financial advisors encourage everybody to be savers and discourage spending, but in fact, we try to help our clients achieve a healthy balance.

People need money to function in our economy, and some of the big spenders we see are among the most astute people we encounter. Some champion savers are unwilling or unable to enjoy life. The "millionaires next door" are often afflicted with one of the saddest

Score Your Risk Acceptance

Are you motivated by greed or by fear? Choose the one number below that best describes how you feel about financial risk. Then mark that number on the vertical scale in Figure 3.1.

1. _____ The most important thing to do with my money is to keep it safe.
2. _____ I believe a bird in the hand is worth two in the bush.
3. _____ Risk-taking often makes me worry.
4. _____ I am generally conservative when dealing with risk.
5. _____ Sometimes I take risks, and sometimes I play it safe.
6. _____ I am generally aggressive when dealing with risk.
7. _____ Sometimes I take risks on impulse.
8. _____ I take big risks but I choose them carefully.
9. _____ I'm willing to take a lot of risk for the chance of a big financial reward.

EXERCISE 3.1

Score Your Saving/Spending Inclinations

Are you a saver or a spender? Choose the one number that best describes how you feel about saving versus spending. Then mark this number on the horizontal spectrum in Figure 3.2.

1. _____ I squeeze every penny I can out of my budget.
2. _____ Use it up, wear it out, make it do, or do without.
3. _____ I'm a very careful shopper and use coupons.
4. _____ I buy quality and rely on brand names.
5. _____ I save 10% of my income.
6. _____ I like to pamper myself with little things.
7. _____ I love to really splurge once in a while.
8. _____ Life is short. Eat dessert first.
9. _____ I spend every penny I get.

EXERCISE 3.2

financial dysfunctions we financial professionals see: the inability to savor the good life they have saved for years to enjoy.

When we add this second dimension, spending propensity, you can see it is a horizontal spectrum running from the obsessive savers on the left to the compulsive spenders on the right. Estimate where you would fit along this spectrum by completing Exercise 3.2, "Score Your Spending/Savings Inclinations," and mark it on Figure 3.2. It is doubtful that you are at either extreme.

Now that you can see where you fit along the two dimensions of the Money Personality Matrix (risk acceptance and saving/spending tendencies), extend the vertical and horizontal lines next to the number that

> **Some champion savers are unwilling or unable to enjoy life. The "millionaires next door" are often afflicted with one of the saddest financial dysfunctions we see: the inability to savor the good life they have saved for years to enjoy.**

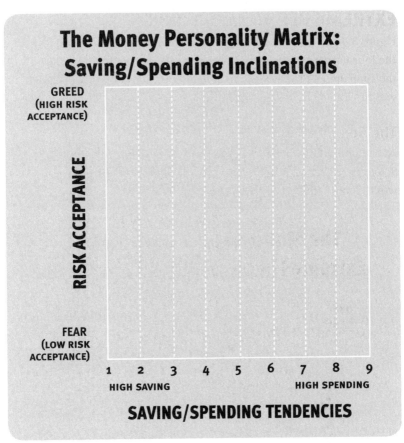

The Money Personality Matrix: Saving/Spending Inclinations

GREED
(HIGH RISK ACCEPTANCE)

RISK ACCEPTANCE

FEAR
(LOW RISK ACCEPTANCE)

1   2   3   4   5   6   7   8   9

HIGH SAVING   HIGH SPENDING

SAVING/SPENDING TENDENCIES

FIGURE 3.2

fits you on each scale to see where they intersect. Find this point on the matrix in Figure 3.3. This will identify your general money personality type in relation to other people.

Believe it or not, with just this simple illustration we can predict and describe many of the sources of financial dysfunction we see in our offices. The extreme cases are the easiest to understand. So let's start by examining the most financially dysfunction-prone money personalities.

EXTREME PERSONALITY TYPES

Figure 3.3 shows the four extreme financial personality types, found in the four corners of the matrix: the scrooge, the gambler, the miser, and the shopaholic. (The large gray diamond in the center of the matrix will be examined later in the chapter.)

The Scrooge

At the upper-left corner is the personality type we call the scrooge. Scrooges are very strongly motivated by a desire to accumulate great wealth (one definition of greed); they also have a strong propensity to save.

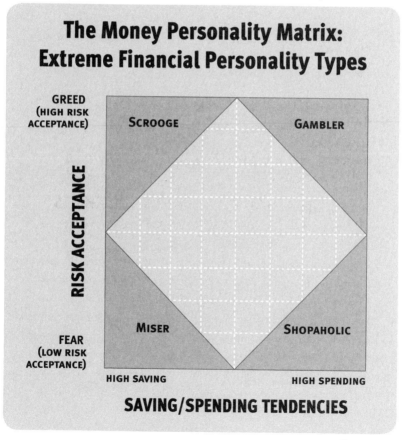

The Money Personality Matrix:
Extreme Financial Personality Types

GREED
(HIGH RISK
ACCEPTANCE)

SCROOGE   GAMBLER

RISK ACCEPTANCE

FEAR
(LOW RISK
ACCEPTANCE)

MISER   SHOPAHOLIC

HIGH SAVING   HIGH SPENDING

SAVING/SPENDING TENDENCIES

FIGURE 3.3

The scrooge personalities we see are frequently very successful businesspeople who have amassed large amounts of money. They tend to be distrustful of others, very concerned about confidentiality, and suspicious of all kinds of financial schemes. They are skeptical of new kinds of financial investments. They tend to find a niche or an approach that allows them to make money, and they like to use it over and over again.

> **At the extreme, you may find scrooges changing their wills on a whim depending on which relative falls into or out of favor.**

Scrooges are susceptible to some very specific kinds of financial blunders. They generally hate to pay taxes, which frequently becomes an area where they make mistakes. Of all the financial mistakes you can make, getting deeply into trouble with Uncle Sam is one of the most deadly.

The scrooge is often a very controlling personality type. At the extreme, you may find scrooges changing their wills on a whim depending on which relative falls into or out of favor. As employers, scrooges tend to surround themselves with people who agree with them. This makes it hard for them to get and process new information about their financial lives.

Sometimes we see dysfunctions in the way scrooges handle their investments. Because they tend to be skeptical, the investments of people with scrooge-like tendencies end up being very concentrated. One client with scrooge characteristics told me his motto for investing: "You put all your eggs in one basket and then you watch that basket very carefully." Unfortunately, that carefully watched basket is subject to the volatility of the market. There are ways to diversify and insulate yourself from the whims of unstable financial markets. They are not hard to learn or to put into practice. But scrooges have to fight their own nature to do this.

When scrooges do try to diversify, they often shun traditional marketable investments, which they perceive as being too uncontrollable (since they are impacted by unpredictable market forces), and not suitable for investors with their superior financial acumen. Instead, they often buy into very high-risk, illiquid private offerings, which they think puts them closer to the action. These are usually in types of businesses they know nothing about, but their past successes may give them a cocky attitude toward investments. The best-known example of this tendency is doctors who are very successful in their practices but have to learn the hard way that success in one field does not necessarily make a person a successful investor. They are sitting ducks for people selling limited partnerships, oil and gas ventures, and so on. Often, successful entrepreneurs or powerful people in politics exhibit scrooge personalities. Examples are Howard Hughes, Ferdinand Marcos, and most of the used-to-be millionaires of the dot.com era.

The Gambler

At the upper-right corner of Figure 3.3 you have the gambler, who is strongly motivated by a desire to be associated with great wealth. Gamblers also have a strong propensity to spend.

This type of personality doesn't often come to see a financial advisor, but we would have to consider the gamblers we do see as addictive personalities. They frequently have heavy debt and often seek help only because they've gotten into trouble with the IRS. Often there is a pattern of alcoholism, substance abuse, or sexual addiction. At the same time they tend to be incorrigible optimists who always believe better days are coming or a better bet is yet to be made. In a remarkable number of cases, they are correct in this assessment when everybody else believes they are wrong. This success simply reinforces their gambling tendencies.

But gamblers can also become remorseful and depressed to the point of suicide because of the mistakes they have made. This leaves them highly vulnerable to the latest get-rich-quick scheme that promises to be the answer to all their financial problems. This type of personality is also prone to become involved in white-collar crime. An extreme case reported in the news involved a loyal employee who started taking undocumented loans from the cash register. These gradually escalated to grand-scale embezzlement. The employee's

> **Gamblers' warped financial logic often results in their viewing the casino or a horse race as a type of investment.**

defense was that she really intended to pay it back—all $2 million!

Gamblers are frequently embarrassed about the way they handle money. They get so good at lying to themselves and others that they actually believe their lies. They brag when they win but seem to ignore and deny their losses. This makes it very hard for them to address their financial issues in a reasonable, logical way. Their warped financial logic often results in their viewing the casino or horse races as a type of investment.

Interestingly, I find that many of these personalities have an inclination to buy into various types of so-called permanent life insurance policies (often called whole life, variable life, vanishing premiums, etc.). This is done at times in the addiction cycle when they feel remorse over their bad habits and want to appear responsible to their family.

One gambler confided to me that after going on a gambling binge he would feel extremely guilty. He would promise himself that he would change his ways. Once a supposed friend who sold life insurance showed up at one of these low points and convinced him he would be a dutiful husband by loading up on life insurance.

Like most life insurance agents, his friend persuaded him that what he called permanent insurance was perfect because it was a form of forced savings. The printouts done by the agent demonstrated what a great investment it was as well. So he bought a $1 million universal life policy with premiums of $20,000 a year. Of course, it was only a matter of a few years before he dropped the policy (as do 80% of those who buy into the permanent life insurance fiasco, since these policies are often sold to unsavvy buyers without adequate liquidity to continue the payments or tie up their savings for 20 or more years). He received virtually nothing for the $40,000 he paid, because the life insurance agent typically is paid the first year's premium as commission!

If you are a gambler and feel the need to buy life insurance to assuage your guilt, do yourself and your family a favor and buy pure level term insurance. This type of insurance doesn't involve an investment scheme and costs a tenth or less of what permanent insurance costs, with much more modest commissions paid to the salesperson.

The Miser

At the lower-left corner of Figure 3.3 is the miser, who is strongly motivated by fear but has a natural inclination to save.

The few true misers we see are champion savers, but they have little to show for it. They are fearful about investments, even straight-forward ones that are simple to explain and understand. At the most extreme, these are the people who keep all their money in a mattress or cans buried in the backyard. More commonly, people with miser-like tendencies hoard their money in bank accounts and Treasury bills. They are afraid of running out of money, so they avoid any kind of long-term financial commitment or a long-term investment that has a long-term payoff.

One miser I worked with in the 1970s had over $100,000 saved up, even though he was only 35 years old. He kept it all in a savings account at the bank earning 2% interest. He was reluctant even to consider anything else because he didn't want to lose his savings. It took two years to convince him to buy U.S. Treasury bills, which then paid 8% and are even safer than FDIC-insured bank accounts because they don't have a maximum limit. Three years later, I finally managed to persuade him to buy a home (he had been renting all this time!).

Sometimes it seems the misers want to punish themselves with denial, as if they don't deserve the more pleasant things in life. Very frequently these people had a childhood that was marked by high money consciousness—they were taught at a very early age to watch every penny and save as much as possible.

Terrible investments that misers, like gamblers, love to lose their money on, include life insurance. Unlike the gambler, however, the miser is motivated by fear rather than guilt. The returns promised by the salesperson can seem convincing because misers generally are not very financially astute, and, of course, the agent always stresses how safe his or her company is.

Usually, the insurance companies that go broke were indeed in good shape 20 years before their demise, when most of their outstanding policies were sold. So it can be a real jolt to misers if their insurance company does go belly-up. Even if the company remains solvent for the next 20 or 30 years and then the policy is cashed in, the miser is also disappointed to find that it would have been better to buy term insurance and invest the difference in U.S. savings bonds.

Because misers don't generally understand key concepts about income taxes, they are easily convinced to buy various types of annuities. These are touted as a tax shelter even though the client may only be in a 15% tax bracket. Misers generally are not sophisticated enough to realize that gains realized in a stock portfolio outside an annuity are taxed at about half the rate that gains are taxed when taken from an annuity.

> The few true misers we see are champion savers, but they have little to show for it.

Even investors who are not naive don't realize that financial salespeople are paid the highest commission on annuities, which accounts for the steep surrender charges (surrender charges are penalties triggered if the investor wants to sell before 5 to 10 years). These charges offset the commissions paid and often mean the total cash returned is less than what was invested in the first place, even if the investments themselves have gone up in value.

Misers tend to be excellent record-keepers but are frequently confused about what kinds of records they need to keep and for how long. They tend to be very afraid of the IRS and would rather pay too much in taxes than run the risk of being audited.

Until the typical miser can overcome the fear of the entire investment process, the money saved is not effectively invested. Thus these personality types cannot grow their financial resources in a way that their savings habits should be making possible. And until they feel comfortable that they are building for the future, they are not able to enjoy the precious days of their lives now. This, it seems to me, is a terrible dysfunction, and whenever we find it, we try to help them solve it as quickly as possible.

The solution for misers almost always is a large dose of education. Once they start understanding the principles of financial growth, they slowly become more willing to expand their portfolio and balance their risks more effectively. Because they are open to financial coaching, misers are usually fast learners and shed their fear in a relatively short time.

The Shopaholic

Finally, in the lower right-hand corner of the matrix shown in Figure 3.3 is the shopaholic, who is motivated by fear and has a strong propensity to spend.

People with shopaholic tendencies are typically the most enjoyable people in the world to spend time with. Friendly and outgoing, they love to give gifts or pick up the tab—just put it on their credit card, please. That one was declined? Well, here—try one of these.

Shopaholics often come from impoverished families and were deprived as children. They confuse their needs with their wants and justify their need to spend by buying for others. They know the salespeople personally, and the salespeople learn to cater to them. Purchasing the item and putting it on their credit card becomes a ritual. They get a type of high during the shopping experience, and when they get home they suffer terribly from postaddictive remorse. It is very common for shopaholics to hide their purchases.

Like gamblers, shopaholics hate to keep records, in part because these records provide clear evidence of their problem. Because they are in denial, they seldom know how much their total debt comes to. They are often behind on the paperwork of life, and they are even further behind in their efforts to maintain their financial health. Until they understand the drug-like effect that spending has on them and learn to control their desire for that particular kind of high, they will always be financially weak. For the shopaholic, financial weakness is hard to bear.

I advised one couple who exhibited classic shopaholic tendencies (the shopaholic usually requires an enabler to continue the addiction). The wife blamed her husband for making her angry, insisting that spending was just a way of venting her anger. Then, whenever the husband would make an outlay of money for equipment for his practice, or tuition for college for his children from a previous marriage, she would go on a whirlwind spree to "get even." "If he can afford those things," she rationalized, "then he should be spending the same amount on me!"

Amazingly, shopaholics often convince themselves that jewelry is an investment (because of the gold and precious stones), which is devastatingly naive. The spread between retail and wholesale prices means that jewelry you buy today would only bring 30 to 40 cents on the dollar if you were to sell it the next day, even if the price of gold went up. Of course, if you can justify jewelry as an investment, it is a short step to justifying your entire professional wardrobe as an investment, too!

Shopaholics at the extreme edge are usually beyond the ability to accept help from a financial advisor. This dysfunction can also be aggravated by a shoplifting addiction. Before accepting as a client someone I know is a severe shopaholic, I require him to begin intensive psychotherapy with a qualified professional. Others who are less extreme shopaholics can often be helped by gaining a grasp of the basic dynamics of this dysfunction. Even keeping track of their debt and spending is a big step toward breaking through their denial. Once they have gotten through their denial, they can make great progress.

MORE COMMON PERSONALITY TYPES

The good news is that you are probably not radical enough to fit any of the extreme types. In our experience, less than 15% of the population falls into these categories. Most of the people we see have a healthier blend of these characteristics, which makes them more likely to achieve and maintain their financial functioning. The more common personality types of clients we advise are shown in the center diamond of Figure 3.4 and described below.

The Entrepreneur

Entrepreneurs are the people who start businesses. They don't mind risk; as a matter of fact, some of our clients seem to thrive on it. Very frequently the child of business-owner parents, the entrepreneur probably started businesses in childhood.

Often, entrepreneurs have a sense of mission about their business. They believe in it and focus their whole life on making this dream

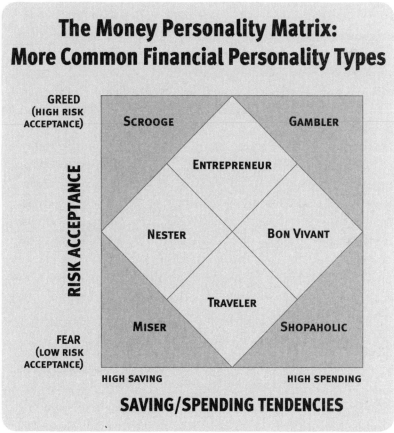

FIGURE 3.4

become a reality. Everything in their life ends up revolving around their business. In the old days, the model was the store owner who lived above his store. That was his home, his business, his whole identity. His wife and children worked for him. So it is for modern entrepreneurs. Their relationships tend to be centered around their business. They choose a relationship or marital partner who has something to contribute to the mission.

Money is their way of keeping score. Like the scrooges, their investments tend to be concentrated in their area of expertise. Inadequate liquidity is their biggest financial problem. They just don't have enough cash to run their businesses properly.

We encourage these people to do what they do well, and we try to take some of the details off their backs. They are capable of enduring wide financial swings that would scare other personality types, and they are able to look at the big picture and the long-term horizon. When they come to us, their financial dysfunction often shows up as overwork and undercapitalization. I highly recommend that they set up lines of credit when times are good and they don't need them, so the money is available when a downturn hits the company.

The other characteristic of entrepreneurs is that they always want to reinvest all their money into their business. They typically ask me why they should "put their money to sleep" buying bonds or risk it buying stock in someone else's company. They believe they are better off with more inventory, equipment, or receivables financing their own business. The truth, however, is that anyone can make money in business when times are prosperous; the businesses that survive long term are those that have a diversified base to enable them to withstand recessions.

Of course, there are exceptions to this pattern. During the bull market of 1996 to 1999, I was surprised at the number of entrepreneurs who finally relented and took money out of their own business to invest in the stock market. Typically, they avoided mutual funds, preferring to trade highly volatile stocks. Then their gains, as well as a good portion of their initial investment, were wiped out in the bear market that began in 2000. This bitter experience did not generally convince them of the virtue of diversification, but rather reinforced their inclination to focus all their investments in their own businesses.

The Nester

Nesters have the ability to save; their favorite investment is their home. Anything nesters buy for their home is regarded as an investment. They don't buy new carpet or new furniture—they invest in it. Anything they buy that isn't for the home is considered somewhat frivolous. If the choice is between a new roof and taking a trip, the house always wins. Something in their house always needs fixing or improving.

In our offices we see many nesters who have overimproved their houses. They buy a little house in a suburban tract, and over the years they add on rooms, dormers, and put in marble countertops. They end up with five bedrooms and all kinds of stuff in the yard. When they sell the house (if they are ever willing to do so), the selling price is never enough to cover the costs of their investment in it. They simply have improved it beyond what the neighborhood justifies. Because many of their improvements actually reflect their own personality peculiarities, the new owner moves in and tears out much of what the nester has done.

Nesters are often very family-oriented with strong religious ties. They are concerned about college education for their children and about their retirement. They tend to be very practical. They are proud of how they handle their money—and, we have found, sometimes defensive about it. If these people come to us in good financial condition, then we help them broaden their investment lives beyond the home.

One of the financial quirks of nesters (although shared by other personalities) is the impulse to pay off their mortgage as soon as possible. They feel safer with their home paid off, even though this is actually a more risky strategy than diversifying beyond their home (see Chapter 4).

Terrible investments that nesters love to lose their money on are buying time-shares and vacation homes. Time-shares virtually never appreciate, and in fact usually sell for 40 to 50 cents on the dollar on the secondary market (i.e., last year's buyers who now want to dump them by running a classified ad in the newspaper). Vacation homes don't make financial sense unless you spend at least thirteen weeks a year there. From a financial standpoint, if you use a vacation home for only a month or two a year, you could rent comparable lodging for less money—even when tax breaks and property appreciation are taken into account.

The Bon Vivant

The bon vivants are the workaholics of the world. They are driven, work long hours, and make a lot of money. Bon vivants spend money on anything that saves them time. Frequently they are called DINKS in marketing parlance: "Double income, no kids." They love gadgets. They love to buy things out of catalogs. If I need advice about how to upgrade the technology in my office, I talk to these people first because they usually are the innovators and early adopters.

People with bon vivant tendencies are concerned about status and prestige, which is the way they reward themselves for their hard work. Brands are important. They also love to give gifts.

When they come into our offices, we find that bon vivants tend to have a very ad hoc investment program. If a bank is giving away airline tickets for opening a certificate of deposit (CD), that CD is in the portfolio. They hear about a stock at a cocktail party and buy some shares. Their portfolio is built a little here and a little there with no guiding overall plan. They are prone to succumb to high-pressure salespeople because they are very open to financial temptations. Too often we see inappropriate high-risk investments owned by people who are low-risk personality types. When the markets go down, they come to see us in acute financial panic.

> A terrible investment mistake that bon vivants make is confusing hobbies with investments.

A terrible investment mistake that bon vivants make is confusing hobbies with investments. For example, one client "invested" several thousand dollars in photography equipment so she could become a professional photographer (even though she had never sold a single photo). Bon vivants even insist that their 28-foot boat is really an investment and its value is sure to go up. In fact, boats, like all manufactured tangible property, never appreciate.

Usually these personalities thrive with financial coaching, as long as they can control their spending. They are anxious to give up the mechanics of their investments and taxes. Bon vivants appreciate the full-service approach of holistic financial advisors because we bring order and continuity to their financial picture. To keep them on track, we always make sure that they check with us before they make investment decisions involving large sums of money.

The Traveler

Travelers prefer to spend money on experiences, rather than things. Generally speaking, they simply don't care about money.

Often, travelers raise antimaterialism to the status of an ideology, and pride themselves on being "downwardly mobile," even bragging about how little "stuff" they have. They love anything that has an educational component to it, and often spend a high percentage of their income on personal growth programs. They always seem to be just one seminar away from happiness. Travelers are the ones who become professional students.

They often enjoy travel and seek out employment situations that call for a lot of time in airplanes. They like a simple life and tend to avoid anything that is going to cause them stress or a lot of worry. Travelers' relationships tend to be very transitory, but they can be extremely loyal to someone who has a great deal of tolerance for their mind-set. It is not uncommon to find them in relationships with nesters.

Often the greatest treasure of the traveler is the photo album of her wanderings. One couple I worked with were die-hard travelers and wanted help figuring out how they could liquidate their home, all their belongings, and reduce everything they owned to a 26-pound backpack. We invested all their money (they actually didn't need much to spend) while they took 2 years off and backpacked around the world. Interestingly, when they returned to civilization, they settled down, had kids, and became nesters!

THE LIMITATIONS OF ANY MODEL

Each of these personality types has advantages and disadvantages. There are very positive parts of each personality that tend to promote their financial health and to benefit society at large. There are also avenues that lead to financial dysfunction.

The chances are that you identify with more than one of these personality types. This is perfectly normal. As any professional—be it medical, psychological, or financial—will tell you, the world is not as simple as our models sometimes make it out to be. The personality types run along a dual spectrum. The personality type displayed may be very situational, so that at times a usually entrepreneurial person could show up as an avid traveler or take up craps at the casino.

This is especially true when you add relationships to the spectrum of people who come into our offices. Relationships can make the personality situation very complicated and the financial diagnosis that much harder.

For example, it's not unusual for a miser personality, especially a woman, to get involved with a gambler. The two find a way to compensate for each other. Usually, the woman in that situation is initially smitten with the boastful risk taker, and ultimately she becomes the enabler. By trying to take care of him, she ends up impoverishing herself. The perfect example is a female client of mine who (without consulting me) withdrew $50,000 from her IRA to give to her boyfriend so he could pay off his gambling debts. He convinced her that if he could pay off these debts, he wouldn't need to gamble anymore. Needless to say, he was back in debt within a year, owing even more.

The bon vivant is a natural for the entrepreneur because they are both workaholics. If the bon vivant can subscribe to the entrepreneur's mission, their relationship can work well. The bon vivant adds depth to the entrepreneur's life, and the entrepreneur values the bon vivant's commitment to the success of the business.

As already mentioned, nesters frequently choose travelers in their personal relationships. Once I met an engineer who summarily dismissed the idea that he was financially dysfunctional. Just by asking a couple of questions about his and his wife's risk acceptance (his was higher than hers) and their spending propensity (he was the saver, she the spender), it was clear that he was the nester and she was the traveler. So I remarked to him that I would expect that they owned a time-share. He was amazed! "How did you know that?" he asked. "We actually own three of them!" Time-shares (or RVs, boats with living quarters, and vacation homes) are the perfect compromise for the traveler and the nester.

Similarly, Imelda and Ferdinand Marcos are the archetype of the scrooge and the shopaholic meshing. She supported his megalomania, and he provided the wherewithal for her to accumulate 3,000 pairs of shoes. Thus it is not uncommon for a person to seek balance by choosing someone whose financial personality type is the exact opposite of his to enable or compensate for his own financial dysfunctions.

That scenario would be complicated enough, but more complicated still is the fact that we see financial dysfunction arising from actions that are exactly opposite of the usual pattern of the people who took them. The scrooge, seeing how much he has at risk, may suddenly decide to pay off his home mortgage. The shopaholic may suddenly decide to purchase a very expensive life insurance policy as a form of "forced savings" and wind up with a very poor investment over the long haul. Or the gambler may decide to buy a lot of U.S. savings bonds.

These investments are completely out of character and can be seen as an attempt to compensate. The person motivated by greed suddenly is overwhelmed by fear and reacts by seeking absolute safety. Or the saver has a brush with death and goes on a spending spree. These impulsive decisions do nothing to address the underlying dysfunctions. They often aggravate the financial problems that clients bring to us for our professional assistance.

> **Before you can take steps to become financially fit, you need to understand who you are and what your personality propensities happen to be.**

As we go through life, it also is common for us to move from one personality type to another as we either mature or learn to cope with the stress factors that shape our personalities. Often, the most well-balanced among us are those who have experienced several or all of the various personality types and now have found a comfortable balance.

Before you can take steps to become financially fit, you need to understand who you are and what your personality propensities happen to be. Begin by spending a few minutes learning more about your natural inclinations, as well as those of your partner. Armed with that knowledge, you are well on your way to achieving financial freedom.

The Symptoms of Financial Dysfunction

> Money is of no value;
> it cannot spend itself.
> All depends on the
> skill of the spender.
>
> —RALPH WALDO EMERSON

Earlier in this book, I told you that my financial practice is more complicated today than it was in the relatively simpler world of 35 years ago. Some of these complexities have to do with the increasing pace of change in our world.

TIMES ARE CHANGING

For example, consider the changing demographics of aging. By the year 2025, a projected near-45% of the U.S. population will be age 45 or older, with that group divided almost evenly between those ages 45 to 65 and those ages 65 and over. In 1940 only 7% of 65-year-olds lived to the age of 90. In 2000 that percentage had increased to 26%—more than threefold!

These kinds of demographic statistics get the attention of professional financial advisors. In the past, a retirement portfolio had to last only a few years. Now it is not uncommon to see people retiring at an age where they have 50 years of life ahead of them after retirement. Planning for 50 years of income is one of the challenges I never imagined having to face in my professional career.

> **By the year 2025, a projected near-45% of the U.S. population will be age 45 or older.**

Longevity has had a dramatic impact on family aging as well. Of those people who reached age 50 in the year 2000, 80% have at least one parent still living, and 27% are blessed with two living parents. In 1950 only 8% of all 50-year-olds had two living parents. For those of us in the financial planning field, this means the nest egg has to be shared in a way we never imagined before.

Over time, we have seen an increase in the percentage of the so-called sandwich generation—middle-aged working people who are supporting both dependent children and dependent parents. The trends are clear in our offices all over the country, and we can see where they are going. In the next decade, we will be reaching the point where those in middle age will, on average, have more parents to support than children!

Thus many people are headed for serious financial problems in their retirement years and don't even realize it yet. I'm concerned that not far in the future financial professionals will be dealing at an increasing rate with clients who have impossible financial problems. I foresee more and more people coming to us with their finances ravaged by decades of financial dysfunction. Lack of planning, combined with ill-informed financial strategies, eventually will build up to the point where these people will be facing economic disaster. After perhaps 30 years in retirement, they will still be supporting an aging parent. More than likely there will be enormous health care costs, and they may run out of money for their own needs.

So what can we do? I think all of us in the financial planning community need to do a better job of helping the general public identify the signs of oncoming financial problems for themselves. Everywhere you look, you see advice from financial columnists, Wall Street analysts, and TV talk show hosts. But very seldom do you hear from the financial advisors in the trenches who help people get on top of their financial situations every day.

SEVEN SYMPTOMS OF FINANCIAL DYSFUNCTION

The good news is that it's not hard to recognize some of the most common symptoms of incipient financial dysfunction. The way medical professionals identify disease is often very straightforward. They look at the symptoms, and many times they recognize the disease by its effects on your body. The process is similar in the financial world as well. Sometimes the symptoms are easy to identify, and sometimes we need to look deeper.

In this section, I share with you the symptoms we often see in people who come into our offices. Here's another bit of good news: Unlike the situation in medicine, when a financially dysfunctional person learns to deal with the symptoms, more often than not the dysfunction eventually goes away.

By now, you probably understand that you are part of your own financial problem. Getting some insight into your personality, which we reviewed in Chapter 3, should give you a clue about some of the deficiencies you have to overcome. In this chapter, we describe several common symptoms caused by these dysfunctions. Financial dysfunction can be grounded on three different levels, depending on how embedded it is: the cognitive level, the belief-system level, or the psychological level.

The easiest of these dysfunctions to work with are the cognitive-level dysfunctions. They are based on incorrect information or a lack of understanding. For example, often people don't realize how much extra things cost when they are financed on a credit card. I tell them that it's like going to tag sale where everything is marked up an extra 20% rather than being marked down. Sometimes this straightforward cognitive approach is sufficient for them to understand why they should pay off their credit cards monthly and they act on this advice. With only a little education, it is relatively easy for you to change your behavior once you understand the reasons behind financial recommendations.

More complicated to overcome are unconscious belief systems, which are usually rooted in learned values from childhood or family of origin. These require reprogramming using a different paradigm (see Chapter 5). Let's return to the example of credit card debt. When the cognitive approach isn't effective, I try to give the client a new paradigm. Consumer debt is a sure sign that people are living beyond their means, that they are trying to be someone they're not. This carries with it a heavy burden of guilt and fear, sapping the joy from life. Often the debtor tries even more desperately to "get happy" by buying more stuff; instead, he becomes increasingly ashamed and scared, and a vicious vortex sets in that can suck him into bankruptcy. Usually, people can change dysfunctional financial behavior when they become aware of a more realistic paradigm, and understand the impact the decisions they have been making are having on their life.

Most difficult to modify are actions based on purely psychological associations. This would be the case if credit card abuse were just the tip of the iceberg, pointing to a full-blown shopaholic. These behaviors are very deep rooted and generally beyond the competence of financial advisors to deal with, although sometimes simple gradual behavior modification can be effective. Financial advisors should refer clients to outside professionals for psychotherapy if the issue is threatening their clients' financial stability.

Each of the symptoms described next can be rooted in the cognitive, belief-system, or psychological level. Different tactics are appropriate to address each symptom, depending on what level it springs from.

Here are the seven symptoms I see most often in my planning sessions:

1. Mortgage aversion
2. Inappropriate risk reactions
3. Compulsive spending or excessive debt
4. Poverty mentality
5. Miser mentality
6. Acute financial paranoia
7. Windfall woes

Before we look at each one of these, a word of caution. This is a general-interest guide to your financial fitness, not a comprehensive textbook delving into all your possible symptoms and dysfunctions. Although these are the most common symptoms we see, many others may be unique to a particular person or be part of a more complicated pattern. A number of financial dysfunctions have not yet been classified. Any general-interest medical book advises you to consult a professional when your situation feels uncomfortable or extreme, or home remedies for the symptoms don't seem to be working. I make the same recommendation here.

Although my list is certainly not intended to be definitive, these are some of the most common symptoms of financial dysfunction. I believe this information will help you recognize what is holding you back from financial freedom.

Symptom #1: Mortgage Aversion

I see mortgage aversion most often among nesters, entrepreneurs, and those who work directly in agriculture. Nesters and entrepreneurs strongly believe that owning their homes free and clear provides a safety net, even though it actually is more risky than having a mortgage, as we will see. Those in agriculture are likely to have family histories of homes and farms lost in the Great Depression. However, most people don't realize that, back then, the money borrowed against farms functioned as "seed money" to plant crops, and took the form of 1-year demand notes, not 30-year amortizable mortgages. Banks may have given farmers a break when the first crop failed, and maybe the second, but by the third year, they foreclosed on the land if the notes were not paid off.

It is not uncommon for me to see clients who are earning a lot of money, in the top tax bracket, living in a home with a fair market value of half a million dollars—and with a $200,000 mortgage at an above-market interest rate. When I suggest that they refinance or pull out additional cash for investment, they are shocked. They tell me they are making double mortgage payments or extra principal payments, and they make statements like "The sooner my house is paid off, the more interest I save."

This is mortgage aversion at the cognitive level—a lack of understanding or a misunderstanding of how mortgage financing works. For this type of financial dysfunction, the misunderstanding often focuses on the math involved.

My first treatment for people with this problem is simply to illustrate and explain the mathematical realities. I understand that it sounds like a great idea to make biweekly mortgage payments in order to pay off your mortgage in 20 years and save over $25,000 in interest. However, the interest savings result from two factors: (1) You are accelerating your payments to the beginning of the month, and (2) you are paying the equivalent of 13 monthly payments each year (based on 26 biweekly periods).

To determine whether or not this is a good deal, you must compare how much your money would earn if you invested it rather than using it to pay off the mortgage. I have crunched the numbers in this scenario for many people, and I have never once found it to be in the borrower's favor. See Table 4.1, "30-Year versus Biweekly Mortgages," for an example of these calculations. In this example, a client has a traditional thirty-year mortgage with a fixed interest rate of 6%, which requires monthly payments of $959. After an initial five-year period, her mortgage company offers (for a $500 fee) to allow her to convert to biweekly payments equal to half her monthly payments, or $480. Since she is paid biweekly, this seems convenient. The highly touted advantage is that biweekly payments will enable her to pay off her mortgage 3 years sooner and save over $25,000 in interest. This looks like a great deal. but after analyzing it, you can see it is a scam. As you can see in Table 4.1, by staying with the 30-year mortgage, she has $959 available to invest each year. After 30 years, the return on that modest yearly investment is $96,925—whereas the amount saved on interest by switching to a biweekly mortgage is only $25,203. By sticking with the 30-year fixed mortgage, the client could use $40,846

30-Year versus Biweekly Mortgages

	BIWEEKLY	30-YEAR FIXED
Original mortgage amount	$160,000	$160,000
Balance of mortgage after 5 years	$148,887	$148,887
Payment amount	$479.64	$959.28
Payments per year	26	12
Payments for a whole year	$12,470.65	$11,511.37
Extra cash available to invest/month	----	$959.28
AT END OF BIWEEKLY LOAN (24.5 YEARS):		
Interest saved using biweekly payments	$25,203	
Amount accrued from extra cash invested	$0	$79,871
Principal amount remaining	$0	$40,846
Net gain with 30-year fixed*		$39,024

*Assumes 30-year mortgage is paid off by investment accrued.

TABLE 4.1

from the accrued investment to pay off the mortgage the same year the biweekly mortgage would be paid off, and still have over $39,000 left!

Sometimes, this comparison is all people need to see, and their financial fitness is restored. They get the lowest possible mortgage rate and they leverage the safest investment they have in their portfolio. But sometimes, they are still blocked from taking the appropriate action. At the unconscious belief-system level, the signal may be a "neither a borrower nor lender be" mind-set or the conviction that paying off the mortgage demonstrates responsibility or financial success. Very frequently, people receive this powerful message in childhood through a mortgage-burning ceremony or by repeated warnings from adults about the evils of all debt.

In these cases, the person needs a new paradigm so he will understand the concepts and theory behind the strategy of keeping a home mortgage. This entails explaining positive leverage, combined with the tax benefits of the mortgage. We can tell him that a 15-year mortgage at 7% interest costs less than 5% after taxes, due to federal tax incentives for homebuyers. Thus he gains positive leverage if he can invest the money that he would have otherwise used to pay down the mortgage at more than 5% over the 15-year period. A mortgage also provides homeowners with additional protection against inflation cycles (see Chapter 7).

Even after understanding this paradigm, however, you may still not be comfortable having 80% of your home mortgaged. It may be a visceral reaction you can't explain, but it is real nonetheless. You understand the math; you understand the theory; but you just can't bring yourself to do it emotionally.

My prescription for action in these cases is to tell you to take small incremental steps in order to desensitize yourself. For example, borrow $50,000 and open a separate brokerage account for that money. If you panic, you can go to that account, sell your investments, and pay off your mortgage. Most clients who are mortgage-adverse in the extreme are willing to try this approach, and I have never had a client cash in the investments to pay off the mortgage, even in down markets!

Symptom #2: Inappropriate Risk Reactions

Inappropriate risk reactions come in two forms: risk aversion (reluctance to invest in the stock market or sabotaging your finances by lack of diversification) or excessive risk exposure (putting money into unsuitable, high-risk ventures).

Let's start at the cognitive level. First you need to understand the basics of investments. Too many of us financial advisors are surprised at the number of people who do not understand the differences between stocks and bonds. Yet when I go for my annual physical and have my blood pressure taken, my physician always needs to explain again the difference between systolic and diastolic and which one is the top number and which is the bottom. Likewise, we try to explain the basic financial distinctions in an uncomplicated way. Yet we know that these basics may need to be reviewed at the next visit, just as my doctor has to reexplain my blood pressure measurements. (In case you are wondering, you can find an explanation of the difference between stocks and bonds on pages 182 to 186.)

At the belief-system level, the driving force may be a fear of punishment for appearing greedy. Entrepreneurs may not understand the need for diversification if they are already doing well in their own business. I find that more advanced financial education works best here, especially regarding something called *modern portfolio theory* (see Chapter 5).

A lack of experience in diversified investments can be solved simply. For some clients, we set up experimental accounts that they can manage on their own. These accounts have a limited amount of funds designated as "Las Vegas money" for those inclined to gamble with high-risk stocks. Then we properly diversify the rest of their assets.

Whenever I offer this solution and set up Las Vegas accounts, I tell my clients that the worst thing that can happen to them is that they will triple their money in the first year. The danger is that they will start thinking they really know what they're doing and want to do more of it. Fortunately, this seldom happens.

Symptom #3: Compulsive Spending or Excessive Debt

High and increasing credit card debt is one of the most common financial dysfunctions in America today. Often, a certain level of denial accompanies it, so you delay seeking help until the problem is overwhelming. You may have no idea how much you owe on your credit cards and be amazed when confronted with the reality.

To a layperson, it might seem that people with credit card debt simply don't make enough money to pay all their bills, which is what some people say right up front. But in all my experience as a financial advisor, I have never seen debt to be in any way related to income. I find people earning hundreds of thousands of dollars a year getting deeper and deeper in debt while others who earn a few tens of thousands are putting money aside on a regular basis.

The solution to compulsive spending or excessive debt requires some work. We start with basic consumer education: how much it actually costs to buy things on credit. We also help you track all your expenditures for a limited period and then help you create a spending plan.

It isn't always that easy, though. Once again, belief systems can get in the way. I had one client with no assets who was over $40,000 in debt because of the way she had interpreted her mother's message: "The most important thing is to have good credit." Every time she received a credit card solicitation in the mail, she understood it to mean she had good credit. So she continued to accept the offers until she could no longer handle the minimum payments required.

You may argue, "I deserve to live like this. All my friends do." If you believe this, benchmarking can help you understand how your belief system is undermining your financial future. The Financial Life Cycle, discussed in Chapter 7, is a helpful tool to help you understand what level of accumulation is congruent with your income level, regardless of what your friends are doing.

In the tougher cases, debt consolidation is appropriate, and sometimes we recommend consumer credit counseling. One mandatory step is to give up the credit cards. In our offices we literally take them away from our clients. This breaks the cycle—the habit—and it also leads to making more conscious decisions about money. I see over and over again that people who abuse credit cards do not think of charging their purchases as spending money. (This is why casinos want you to gamble with chips, so you're not aware that you're spending money, by the way.) Having to use real money again instead of plastic helps you get back in touch with cash and with your spending habits. Most people are able to return to using credit cards after a period of time, although many choose not to.

At the psychological level, credit cards can be a true addiction with all the accompanying addictive traits. Often, there is a history of childhood deprivation. If your addiction has already affected you financially, major lifestyle adjustments may be in order. However, the primary prescription for action is a referral for psychological therapy, which can provide specialized services beyond the scope of a financial advisor's expertise.

Symptom #4: Poverty Mentality

You may suffer from poverty mentality if you earn substantially below your capability and you're always broke. We hear people with this problem tell us, "This is all the market will pay in my area," or "My company only gives 3% raises."

In treating this problem, we start by providing benchmarks. You need a way to measure how you're doing. You can easily find statistical information on compensation for various professions on the Internet. If others are earning this amount working for other companies, why can't you earn this amount from your employer?

At the belief-system level, statements like "Rich people make other people poor," or "Money is the root of all evil," or "If I charge more, the people who need me won't be able to afford me" are sure signs of the poverty mentality. I have even heard these beliefs expressed by other financial advisors!

> **You may suffer from poverty mentality if you earn substantially below your capability and you're always broke.**

The reality, whether we agree with it or not, is that money is the way our society values things. People pay money for what they value—whether it be cigarettes, education, medical services, or financial planning. When people are undercharged for a product or service, they value it less; that is, they discount it. As a result, clients of professionals who undercharge are often late, don't show up for appointments, or fail to follow through on recommendations. Properly pricing your work ensures that people properly value the service you are performing. Overcoming the poverty mentality rewards you with a host of financial benefits and a boost to your self-esteem. In addition, your clients will be more motivated to take your professional advice and to implement your suggestions.

If you have too much business to handle, it's a sure sign that you are underpriced. If you're resistant to raising your fees, raise them only for new clients. Once you see that many people out there will acknowledge the value of your service by paying this higher rate, it becomes easier to raise fees for current clients as well.

Symptom #5: Miser Mentality

Miser mentality is the flip side of the poverty mentality. You may have more money than you will ever spend in your lifetime and yet find that you are unable to give yourself permission to spend. This problem is not a function of how much money you have; it's a function of how much you spend in relation to what you have.

When we educate our clients, we show them that using investment income does not deplete their savings. But not everybody can hear this message clearly. Many people have heard other messages: "A penny saved is a penny earned" or "If I spend too much, my friends won't like me." But if they continue living the way they are living, all they are doing is making Uncle Sam their largest beneficiary.

At the psychological level the miser usually has a fear of being different from friends and neighbors—a fear of what someone earlier in the person's life may have described as "showing off." The miser mentality especially affects people who live in tightly knit communities or small towns. What is most effective in these cases is a clearly defined, controlled splurge. For example, fly first-class for just one trip. Or, to motivate yourself, invest in memories: Take the grandkids on a trip.

Symptom #6: Acute Financial Paranoia

We see acute financial paranoia either on a personal level (e.g., people who are always afraid that they will be sued) or on a global level (e.g., the Y2K frenzy and the steep increase in the price of oil). If you suffer from acute financial paranoia, you may believe that in order to survive you should transfer your assets to your spouse (or offshore) or build and live in a bunker.

Believe it or not, many of us in the financial planning field are willing to cater to these fears—up to a point. We help you understand about exempt assets or the protection from creditors available to you under the law. Some of you may need a better understanding of the function of liability insurance. Or you may simply not make enough money to make it worthwhile for someone to sue you.

At the belief-system level, the fear derives from a sense of eventual punishment for success. Some people live their whole lives waiting for the rug to be pulled out from under them. So I stress that financial planning is a process, not an event. It is not something we do once and then we're on our own. You will meet regularly with your financial advisor, planning for contingencies and dealing with unforeseen events as they occur. Because the truth is you never can rule out the risk of unforeseen events.

Symptom #7: Windfall Woes

The symptoms of windfall woes can take many forms, depending on the source of the windfall. When the source is an inheritance, you may experience feelings of guilt, a fear of death, and increased sibling rivalry. When people win the lottery, they fear becoming the target (potential victim) or victim of exploitation. The source may be stock options that paid off big (Silicon Valley syndrome), a large divorce settlement, or a substantial settlement from a lawsuit.

Interestingly, a windfall magnifies all our underlying dysfunctions. If we felt guilty about money to start with, we really feel guilty when Mom dies. If we are afraid and paranoid about money, receiving money does not solve the paranoia—we simply become more afraid and paranoid.

If you receive a windfall, we usually recommend a cooling-off period of anywhere from 6 months to 2 years. We advise clients to leave the money in a money market fund, and during that time we focus on financial education. You may be embarrassed at first about your windfall. You may be inclined to give it away or otherwise make sure it doesn't remain in your life. You may be compelled to comply with stated or unstated family expectations. As a result, you may give inappropriate gifts—with an aftermath of anger, resentment, or depression.

Sometimes no cure exists for this ailment. I had a client once who was cursed with both annual income from a trust fund and the expectation of a large inheritance upon the death of her grandfather. In today's dollars, her annual income from the trust was about $75,000. She found this amount could easily pay rent on adequate housing with plenty left over for partying and, in particular, drugs. I often wondered what she might have been able to accomplish had she not had that certainty of wealth—had she been forced to find out what her true abilities were and to make a contribution to the world.

SELF-EXAMINATION

The medical professional is always debating whether patients should be encouraged or even allowed to self-diagnose. But I think a certain degree of self-diagnosis is every person's right and responsibility, for both our physical health and our financial health. When people come into our offices, they are often unable to recognize their own symptoms and they don't realize that the cures for these symptoms are fairly straightforward and simple.

If you have made a commitment to better financial fitness, you will better understand your personal financial tendencies. At this point, if you know what type of money personality you are and you understand some of the symptoms of financial dysfunction, you are way ahead of the game. Financial freedom is just around the corner!

Tailoring Your Finances to Your Situation

> It is wealth
> to be content.
>
> —LAO TZU

I have already described certain financial dysfunctions and how you can recognize and treat them. Next we're going to focus on how to achieve financial fitness by learning and practicing smart financial behaviors. This requires a major paradigm shift from an exogenous view of financial affairs to an endogenous approach to your money.

An *exogenous* view of the world is the unstated assumption that activities outside yourself are controlling your financial future. These factors include whether the stock market is going up or down, or whether the Federal Reserve will raise interest rates, or what the next calamity will be in the world. You have no control over these factors, and compared to the impact that endogenous factors exert on your life, exogenous events are merely contextual.

An *endogenous* approach, by contrast, focuses on the impact of the things that happen in your life. They include education, marriage, children, occupation, disability, divorce, and layoffs. These are the real issues that your financial plan needs to address.

Financial dysfunction is usually caused by an exogenous orientation. In my experience as a financial professional, most people could avoid the most common financial dysfunctions altogether if they knew more about how to do it. In addition, the great news is that it's not that difficult, time-consuming, or complicated to do. First, be very careful who you listen to. Financial quackery is the primary breeder of exogenous outlooks. To avoid quackery you must recognize the quacks—financial people who are anxious to give you advice but who aren't as concerned about your financial goals as they are about their ability to meet their own sales goals. The unhappy truth in my profession is that the vendors have created much of what passes for theory in the financial planning world.

Mutual fund companies, life insurance organizations, information providers, and discount brokerage houses make their living by feeding (sometimes greedily) off your financial nest egg. Some of these organizations should be charged with financial malpractice. Although certain products are appropriate in their place, in many cases their solutions are not offered with your financial goals in mind.

Of course, we can find the same basic dynamic in other professions. Much of what is available in Western allopathic medicine is really a product of the pharmaceutical companies defining, creating, and selling their products and treatments. Sometimes you will find medical equipment manufacturers defining surgical approaches or insurance companies defining the standard of care. In recent years, much of the science and art of healing has been taken out of the hands of physicians and is being molded or dictated by industry sources. We could write an entire book about this, but in my opinion having organizations other than doctors design medical treatments or decide how best to treat patients has not resulted in better patient care.

In the medical world, we are seeing an increased demand for holistic medicine. This desire for a new approach begins with the recognition that the mind and the body are intimately connected and that healing starts with choosing to create and maintain a healthy lifestyle. Exactly the same thing is true of financial health. The good news is that maintaining financial health is much easier than maintaining medical health, where you are subject to a variety of plagues, accidents, and the wear and tear of normal living.

Let's look at some of the things you can control about your financial life. You might be surprised at how much control you have. Exercise 5.1, "Your Control over Your Financial Fitness," provides a quick self-test of how you perceive your financial fitness.

If you selected any of the answers from Column A in Exercise 5.1, you aren't yet fully in control of your own financial fitness, because, in each case, the correct answer is in Column B.

ASSET ALLOCATION

For one thing, you have a great deal of control over the volatility that your portfolio will experience when the markets go up and down. You

Your Control Over Your Financial Fitness

To see how much control you have over your financial fitness, let's take a little quiz. Which of the following do you think will most impact your financial future?

COLUMN A		COLUMN B
Interest rates	or	Taxes
The specific investments you choose	or	The diversification of your investments across all asset classes
Inflation	or	Being a wise shopper
Technology	or	How much you earn
The political climate	or	The stability of your relationships
Globalization	or	The home you purchase
The rate of return on your investments	or	How much you save for retirement

EXERCISE 5.1

> **A wise investor's portfolio is created with a variety of different asset classes, mixed together according to the characteristics of each one.**

can even make money in years when all your friends are losing their shirts. This is not done by timing markets (discussed in detail in Chapter 8), but by making sure that your assets are properly allocated in relation to your stage in life and the amount of risk appropriate in your particular situation.

It is sometimes hard to explain these concepts to the financial layperson, but after 35 years, I have found a way to make some of the principles clear. When we talk about investment portfolios, the most common question people ask is this: "How high a rate of return can I get?" Surprisingly, from an endogenous standpoint, this is exactly the wrong question to ask. The real question is this: "How much risk is appropriate for my stage in life, and what kind of return is reasonable to expect with a balanced portfolio?"

THE JOURNEY

Suppose we view your investment progress as a journey. You want to fly, let's say, from Detroit to Los Angeles. To get there you could go and talk to a fighter pilot who specializes in very fast trips—the equivalent of a very high yearly rate of return. The fighter pilot will tell you how big his engines are and talk knowledgeably about the jet stream winds. He'll tell you how he can maneuver quickly up and down to different altitudes and that he knows how to squeeze every second out of the duration of the trip. If all goes well, he can get you there in two hours and fifteen minutes.

This person may or may not tell you about the high cost of traveling in his plane or the risks involved. At one point, according to statistics cited by Tom Wolfe in *The Right Stuff*, roughly 25% of all the pilots of the new fighter aircraft eventually crashed and burned.

If you talk with a competent fee-only personal financial advisor, you will be told that going with the fighter pilot involves substantially more risk than you should be taking on what is basically a routine trip. We go to Los Angeles regularly using a commercial jetliner and we know the way. We don't try to set speed records, but we pay attention to how comfortable your seat is, the safety of your flight, what dinner you'd like, and the movie you'll enjoy. We try to assure you of the smoothest ride possible. It may take us four hours and thirty minutes to get you there, but we're not worried about that because getting there quickly is not as important as getting there safely—and making sure that you enjoy your trip.

The smoothness of our investment trip, as it were, is defined by what we in the profession call asset allocation, a concept whose principles were developed by some famous economists, including F. W. Sharpe and Harry Markowitz. These men (along with Merton Miller) won the Nobel Prize for economics in 1990 for the concept of modern portfolio theory. In essence, modern portfolio theory states that you can actually lower the risk and increase the rate of return on your investment portfolio by not putting all your investment eggs in one basket. A wise investor's portfolio is created with a variety of different asset classes, mixed together according to the characteristics of each one.

RISK AND REWARD

The principles of this process are not that difficult to grasp. Most people understand that return is a reward for risk. As shown in Figure 5.1, if you take a very low amount of risk, you will end up with a very low return on your investment. Conversely, if you are receiving a high rate of return on any investment, you are inevitably taking a high amount of risk.

This is especially true when dealing with efficient markets— markets with many informed participants who react quickly to new information. Financial markets are considered the most efficient and competitive of all markets.

This is why whenever people think they have found an incredibly good deal, there are usually risks related to the investment that they are not taking into account. For example, clients often ask my advice about various bonds that pay above-market yields. There is always a good story to go with the bonds—perhaps it's for a church or it is short term to sponsor a popular event. When I look into them, I generally find that the issuer does not have audited financial statements and the bonds are unrated and uninsured. This doesn't really qualify as an investment; it's a gamble.

Modern portfolio theory represents a big leap forward in basic investment theory. This theory demonstrates that although the risk/reward model just described is adequate for any single investment, when you put investments

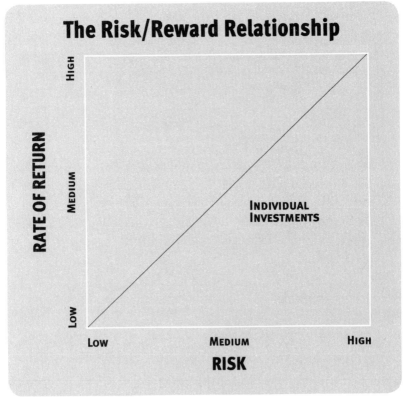

The Risk/Reward Relationship

FIGURE 5.1

together in a portfolio, the risk/reward can be seen as an elliptical curve (see Figure 5.2). Notice the curve in the lower-left quadrant of the figure. The return on investment actually increases while the risk in the portfolio decreases or remains constant when the portfolio is properly diversified.

Unfortunately, most investment solutions for poorly designed portfolios were not created with people like you and me in mind. The most common asset allocation models were designed for huge pension funds and mammoth institutional accounts. They are completely inadequate to address the needs of the individual investor—particularly the middle-income individual investor.

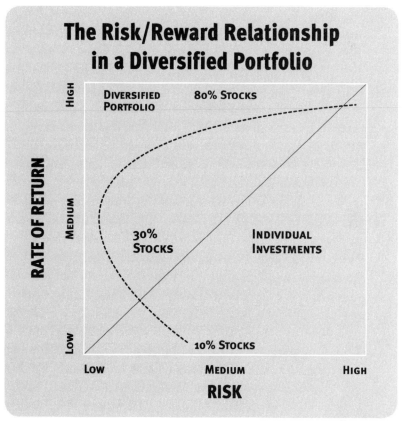

FIGURE 5.2

Here are five major drawbacks to the asset allocation models typically used in the financial planning industry:

1. They include asset classes not applicable to most people, such as foreign bonds and precious metals. The major thrust of many asset allocation models seems to be that a portfolio should mirror the distribution of assets around the world. From a functional standpoint, for real people with real families, this scenario just doesn't make sense. It may be that 6% of the world's wealth is in real estate. But it would be folly to expect a family to have a passable financial plan with only 6% of its marketable assets in real estate.

2. They ignore real estate or at least the personal residence category of real estate. For most middle-income Americans, real estate (particularly in the form of their personal residence) represents their largest single investment. It is probably the best investment that we make in our whole life. In addition, real estate serves a function within the overall asset allocation that cannot be duplicated by any other asset class or category. Properly leveraged, your home functions as your best defense against inflation (we'll discuss why in Chapter 8). It is also the only investment from which you can derive personal enjoyment. To devise asset allocation strategies that completely ignore this asset class is comparable to a physician's designing a treatment plan without ever addressing the patient's diet.

3. They disregard the impact of individual income taxes. The impact of income taxes on an individual's portfolio simply cannot be ignored. Depending on your tax bracket (federal plus state), the government takes up to 45% of your return on some investments every year. On other investments, the government takes up to 40%

only at the end of a certain period of time. The same investment held in a different vehicle can mean the government takes only 20% over a period of time. And on still other investments, the government assesses no tax at all. The market does adjust the rate of return on some investments to compensate for tax consequences, which is why municipal bonds (bonds issued by a city or state) usually pay a lower yield than taxable bonds. But with investment vehicles like the Roth IRA (which can earn money tax free) now available, it is financially foolish *not* to take into account the tax treatment of different investment vehicles.

4. **They disregard functionality.** By disregarding the dimension of functionality, asset allocation models ignore the real-world fact that individuals need certain amounts of liquidity to rely on in the short term. They also must be able to survive long periods of economic downturns. A portion of their portfolio needs to protect them against deflation, a portion against inflation, and a portion must be invested long term to take advantage of periods of prosperity.

> **The impact of income taxes on an individual's portfolio simply cannot be ignored.**

5. **They don't take into account the additional flexibility needed by individuals whose investment horizon is shortened by unforeseen events like death, divorce, disability, displacement from the work force, and so on.** Finally, the asset allocation models in use today were not designed for individuals, but for institutions. Institutional investing is generally driven exogenously by very sophisticated financial strategies that shift asset classes to reflect current market conditions. Individual investing requires an endogenous model that reflects an individual's needs, in which asset class shifts are driven by changes in the stages of the Financial Life Cycle (see Chapter 7).

YOUR FINANCIAL PLAN

An aspect of your financial life entirely in your control is your financial plan. But first you have to know what you're looking for.

Unfortunately, whenever I use the term *financial plan*, it means different things to people who have been subjected to financial quackery than it does to our clients. Thousands and perhaps millions of people have gone to somebody who offers financial advice to the public. They take their financial information and feed it all into a "black box." Out of the other side of the box comes *the plan*—a neatly bound volume filled with printouts, charts, graphs, and projections for the next 10, 20, 30, 40, 50, 60, or more years.

Many of the so-called financial consultants or financial planners who create these plans do not follow the standard professional model. We see many cases where they do not offer advice purely in the client's interest or fulfill the fiduciary's ethical mandate to act in the client's best interests. They are salespeople, not fiduciaries. Life insurance companies pioneered the use of the "book," or "plan," to justify their sales pitch that people need more life insurance. The whole composition of the plan was spreadsheets and assumptions that showed eventually, no matter what, that you were going to run out of money to accomplish what you wanted, so you should buy more life insurance. Imagine if a doctor prescribed only one remedy for every illness and took a commission on that remedy! Wouldn't that be considered the worst form of malpractice?

> **The asset allocation models in use today were not designed for individuals, but for institutions.**

Much of the financial advice given out by plausible-sounding professionals is essentially boilerplate. Everything you get in your "book" is basically the same as everything everyone else gets in their "book." Yes, the numbers are different and your name is printed on every page, but it lacks the integration and flexibility required when dealing with real life.

Let's use the example of saving to send your child to college. The typical financial plan identifies the projected cost of your child's education and calculates how much you must save per year at a given rate to reach that goal. It may provide you with several different scenarios: private versus public college, possible sources of financial aid, and the effects of available tax credits on financial aid.

Instead of "saving for college," I advise clients to save their money in the most tax-efficient vehicle that can help balance their asset allocation.

However, the reality is that no one knows what the opportunities are going to be 20, 10, or even 5 years from now in terms of the options to fund college expenses. Look at the differences between 20 years ago and today! There were no provisions allowing you to borrow from your 401(k) twenty years ago. You couldn't cash in your IRA without penalty for education use. The concept of borrowing against your house to pay for college was not an accepted practice. Education IRAs and state-run Section 529 plans hadn't been invented. You couldn't buy U.S. savings bonds to finance a college education. These are all strategies that you can use today!

Instead of "saving for college," I advise clients to save their money in the most tax-efficient vehicle that can help balance their asset allocation. When their child goes to college, current earnings, scholarship or grant programs, or the child's own earnings may cover the costs—or we will withdraw funds from the most efficient source at that time. This strategy could be borrowing against their house, cashing in savings bonds tax free, borrowing from a 401(k), or taking out a student loan.

I have a client who is a physician with only $250,000 in her pension plan because of part-time work and a disastrous divorce. It's time to send her children to college, and she came to me worried that she could no longer fund her pension because she needed to pay college costs. My advice was simple—and very different from the usual advice you see dispensed by people in my profession: "The government will lend money for your children's education. The government *will not* lend money for your retirement!"

This approach is not accepted wisdom in the financial planning business. However, it was the best advice for her in that particular time and place. The boilerplate advice—to use her retirement funds to pay for her child's college education—would not have helped her reach her goal of financial independence.

YOUR INCOME

Is your income really under your control? For most people who walk into our offices, the answer is "no." But for most of them it could be— and eventually becomes so.

The most limited resource any of us have is our time. Each of us has 24 hours a day. I believe that when we say all people are created equal, what we mean is that we each get 24 hours a day. What we do with our 24 hours a day pretty much determines what kind of life we will have. For many of our clients, an important question we ask early in the relationship is this: "How can you best use the time you are allocating toward generating income to maximize the value of your time?"

To answer this question, realize that every person—whether an entrepreneur or an employee—is compensated based on the value she adds. Entrepreneurs add this value to their clients and investors through their business activities. An employee's value is based on the value he adds to his employer. However, most of us do not look at the job or tasks we do in light of how we can add value more effectively to our employer or to the people we are serving. As a financial planning professional, I see people every day who are not pricing themselves adequately or who are not packaging the services they provide to add the maximum amount of value possible.

I find this particularly true in the digital workplace, where the value of what we add tends to be commoditized. A service becomes commoditized when it can no longer be differentiated qualitatively, so that price becomes the only basis of competition. For example, barbers are commoditized and compete primarily on the basis of price. "Hair Stylists" add a perceived value to their niche market through the quality of their work. Is it true that services frequently can only be differentiated by their price? Consider the illustration shown in Figure

5.3, which I call the Tree of Knowledge. The roots are *data* and the trunk is the accumulation of data, which comprises *information*. Raw data generally becomes useful only after it is analyzed and converted to information. Information, when applied, becomes branches of knowledge. The leaves of the tree, which are the most visible part, are *wisdom*. Applying knowledge successfully, integrating it into particular situations, requires wisdom, which comes in large part from experience.

For many professions, computers and the Internet have taken over the role of accumulating data, analyzing it, and turning it into information. If you are trying to function at the data-accumulation level, it is almost impossible to add value to your employer or client. If

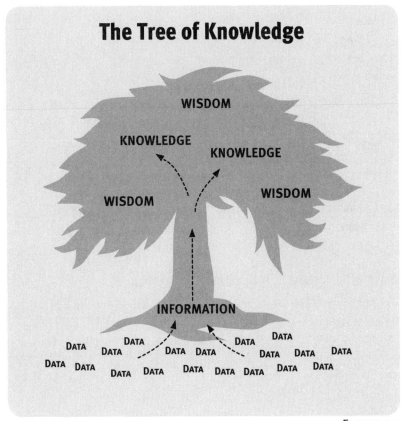

The Tree of Knowledge

WISDOM

KNOWLEDGE

KNOWLEDGE

WISDOM

WISDOM

INFORMATION

DATA DATA DATA DATA
DATA DATA DATA DATA DATA DATA
DATA DATA DATA DATA DATA
DATA DATA DATA DATA DATA DATA DATA DATA

FIGURE 5.3

you take steps to become more skilled, educated, or credentialed in your field, and move up the tree to the knowledge level, you will begin to create value. As you grow, you will also be competing against a large pool of others who are also comparably qualified.

The way to break out from the pack and create value for which you are adequately compensated is to work in the wisdom area of the tree. If you are not charging enough, you are not earning enough. This reality is inevitably the weakest point of your whole financial life—the place where financial dysfunction often begins. I have a client who works as a psychotherapist. When he first came in to see me, he believed that therapists made $85 an hour. As long as he believed that, he was living in an exogenous financial world and letting the external factors control his life.

I questioned his belief and challenged him to look at the value of what he was providing. The focus of his work was men going through midlife crisis. This was an area in which he could bring tremendous value to his patients, but he needed to create a new endogenous pricing model based on this value. What we eventually came up with was a packaged program designed for middle-aged men. His package incorporated group sessions, individual counseling, books, and a weekend retreat to drum and howl at the moon. He marketed it as a program that used midlife crisis as the gateway to the age of maturity and a new appreciation of life. He charged $3,000 for the program and was wonderfully successful. But to get there he had to focus on the value he provided to his patients, not the hourly amount he charged.

APPROPRIATE RISK EXPOSURE

You can exert some control over your own risk exposure and become a more efficient investor. Remember the analogy of the fighter plane versus the commercial jetliner? Both may get you to your ultimate destination, but one offers substantially more risk than the other. At the other end of the spectrum, we see people who are uncomfortable taking to the air at all. They want to ride to their retirement in the financial equivalent of a train or a car, or, if these feel too risky, to simply walk.

Sometimes it is possible to take a slower investment vehicle and get to retirement on time. But with most of the people who come into my office, this is not the case. The number of financial obligations they face in the future is potentially overwhelming unless they take the fastest, safest route to get there—the equivalent, in our analogy, of a commercial jetliner that has an excellent safety record.

So much nonsense on the subject of risk tolerance is out there in the world of financial planning that I hardly know where to begin. For starters, recognize that there are people who will give you a questionnaire and, depending on your answers, will decide whether you belong in a fighter jet, a commercial airliner, a car, or a wagon train.

The whole concept of risk tolerance, in fact, was determined by the stockbroker-wire house industry. This was at a time in the late 1980s when many brokers started being sued for putting too much of their customers' money into risky stocks or illiquid real estate limited partnerships. To shield themselves from liability, they began having their customers take tests to determine their supposed risk tolerance.

I cannot speak for all legitimate financial advisors, but in our practice we regard the use of these tests as measuring devices as a sham—they are neither reliable nor valid. The whole concept of risk tends to be highly situational. I have clients who absolutely refuse to invest in the stock market but think nothing about betting $500 or $1,000 on a roll of the dice at the craps table. Others can't stand the thought of losing money in a casino, but have no problem investing $50,000 or $100,000 in illiquid, speculative private placement ventures that have a very low probability of success and a long time frame to determine whether they will be profitable or not.

Even the concept of risk tolerance is virtually irrelevant to your appropriate asset allocation. If you were going to see a doctor and needed radical surgery, would you want your treatment determined by some unreliable paper-and-pencil test of how much pain tolerance you have? Advisors who rely on this tool are trying to cover their liability exposure by ducking one of their key responsibilities.

The financial advisor's responsibility is to work with clients to determine how much risk they will absolutely have to take to achieve

What's Your Appropriate Risk Exposure?

Your appropriate risk exposure has much more to do with who you are than what can (and will) happen to your investment portfolio. You can read over this list of issues and pretty well determine how aggressive you should be with your investment portfolio.

1. How much do you save? (The more money you save, the more risk you can expose yourself to because you are better able to react to adverse results.)

2. What other risks are you currently taking? How stable is your employment? Do you own your own business? (Also consider other risks you're taking in your life to determine how much risk to take in the investment portfolio.)

3. How much knowledge do you have of investments? (Generally it is appropriate for you to take more risk in areas where you are more knowledgeable.)

4. How much experience do you have in investing? (As events of 2001–2002 showed, many people who had never experienced a down market suddenly discovered their "risk tolerance" was much less than the tests had indicated.)

5. Does your current portfolio provide sufficient protection against inflation?

6. Does your current portfolio provide sufficient protection against deflation?

7. Do you have a spouse who is dependent on you?

8. Are your children dependent on you, and do you plan to pay for their college education? (The more continuing responsibilities people have to other people, the less risk is appropriate in a given financial situation.)

9. What is your emotional tolerance to risk? That is, how do you react to volatility in your portfolio?

10. How much risk is needed to meet your financial goals? (It doesn't make any sense to continue to take risks if you've already won the game!)

EXERCISE 5.2

the important goals in their lives. Some people actually can take less risk and still achieve the life they want. Others need to take more risk—and need more information on how to handle that risk (see Exercise 5.2, "What's Your Appropriate Risk Exposure?").

Giving financial advice in a generic book format is always risky, and here you should pause and realize the possible danger of relying too heavily on this short list. For example, your health and the health of the family are factors in determining how much risk you should be taking. In any situation, the factors cited in the self-test are surely not equally weighted. This is not an engineering exercise.

Here's the point: The risk in your investment portfolio should be congruent with other risks and responsibilities in your life. You have more control over your ability to travel quickly toward your financial destination than you realize. And be sure to ignore anybody who tells you that you need to get there in a big hurry, or that your psychological makeup makes it impossible to travel as quickly as you need, no matter what the tests say.

INFORMATION AND KNOWLEDGE

You can control how well you understand the way your finances and investments work. Surprisingly, in many cases the best advice we can offer is that our clients spend less time—not more—on gathering financial information.

Misinformation

It is hard for any responsible financial advisor not to be embarrassed and a little alarmed at the amount of financial quackery that passes for advice in magazines and investment programs on TV. These are seen and read by millions of people—many of whom are already showing the signs of financial dysfunction. Following

It is hard for any responsible financial advisor not to be embarrassed and a little alarmed at the amount of financial quackery that passes for advice in magazines and investment programs on TV.

the advice offered by these sources often makes the problem worse. Let's start by getting a better understanding of why these information providers are in the business to begin with and what their agenda is.

Before I launch into a tirade about the media, I do want to give credit to the many journalists who have provided a great service to our country and our economy by pointing out conflicts of interests, abusive business practices, and self-dealing in our financial markets. They often publish these criticisms at great risk because their targets are large financial corporations, often the same companies that are heavy advertisers in publications and on television, who use that clout to protect their interests.

That said, I consider the vast majority of the financial information provided by the media to be the equivalent of financial pornography: It gets you all excited, but leaves you feeling dissatisfied, confused, and discontent. Sexual pornography creates unrealistic expectations based on its lurid portrayal of sex as easy to get. Financial pornography offers similar promises regarding money. Obviously, the goal of the print media is to sell its publications, and the goal of television and radio is to sell its advertising time. To do so, information needs to be not only exciting, but it must also appeal to and be deemed relevant by a large audience. In addition, it must convince readers that its advice will make them rich.

> I consider the vast majority of the financial information provided by the media to be the equivalent of financial pornography: It gets you all excited, but leaves you feeling dissatisfied, confused, and discontent.

By its very nature, the media is in the business of convincing you that your financial condition depends on exogenous factors. Something "out there" is happening that you need to know about ("Stay tuned—details at 11"). Worse, it is also in the business of convincing you that the information it provides today, or this hour, will somehow turn you into a successful investor. As it happens, the opposite is actually true: People who act on supposedly hot tips or fund-of-the-month recommendations not only pay more in trading costs. They also pay higher taxes and are far more likely to buy high and sell low than the buy-and-hold investor who simply ignores all the white noise the media spews out for public consumption.

The very basic principles of financial fitness are completely ignored by the media. "Buy and hold," "invest for the long term," "minimize your trading costs" are not headlines that attract subscribers or please advertisers. To accomplish their goal of selling as many copies or advertising slots as possible, the media tends to overemphasize short-term profits or so-called hot stocks.

If you want a simple illustration, here's a list of cover stories from a well-known monthly consumer financial magazine, over just a 12-month period:

- "Funds to Sell—and Why"
- "8 Strategies to Improve Your Returns Now" and "5 Safe Stocks"
- "How to Build the Perfect Portfolio" and "12 Core Funds/10 Solid Stocks"
- "The Right Way to Invest Now"
- "10 Best Funds to Buy Now"
- "13 Top Stocks and Funds to Buy Now"
- "Great Stocks for This Market" and "Best Year-End Moves"
- "Retire Rich! Our Exclusive 60-Minute Plan"
- "Today's Hottest Tech Stocks" and "10 Great Investors"
- "7 Best New Funds"
- "Midyear Investing Special: Blue Chips to Buy"
- "Hot Tech 'Smart Bonds'"
- "The Ultimate Retirement Guide"

If you were to attempt to dutifully follow the advice heralded on the cover of popular financial magazines, switching around your investments monthly to implement their financial prescriptions, your portfolio would be a total shambles in less than a year.

What about a newsletter that does not accept advertising? Even here, you have the same problem; the sales of these newsletters invariably depend on how astute their readers perceive them to be in forecasting market moves. As such, the newsletters are invariably geared toward an exogenous framework.

Can you imagine a newsletter editor selling a monthly edition that month after month basically urges readers not to sell their stocks or bonds and recommends that they buy index mutual funds and government securities? In fact, this is essentially the approach called for from an endogenous standpoint, but it's a lousy formula for pulling in subscription dollars or advertisers.

The Guru Myth

Probably the biggest and most obvious lie promulgated by the media is that someone out there can truly predict what is going to happen next in the financial markets—and if you can just find that person, your financial future will be assured.

Don't you think that if this were true, those in the know would keep that information to themselves? If there were really a fabulous hidden investment opportunity out there, would people be inclined to share it? If some guru could predict market trends and shared the secret, it would soon become widely known and everyone would be using the secret approach. Then it would no longer predict the direction the market would take because it would be discounted.

Yet, repeatedly, people walk into our offices holding the tattered remnants of their nest egg. They had listened to the advice of some investment guru who had made a string of accurate market calls, but who, after they bought a subscription to his newsletter, turned out to be disastrously wrong in the next few calls. How can somebody develop a track record of calling future events and then suddenly lose this ability to predict the next turn of the market?

The phenomenon of the market guru is easily understandable if you consider the theory of large numbers. Here is how I demonstrate it during one of my financial seminars. I have everyone in the room stand up. I have a coin in my hand, and I ask for everyone who predicts that the flip of the coin will be heads to raise their hands. I flip the coin and everyone who predicted wrong has to sit down. I continue this process until only one person is left standing, and then I proceed to have that person guess each flip of the coin.

> **If there were really a fabulous hidden investment opportunity out there, would people be inclined to share it?**

Let's say we start with 40 people, and 20 sit down the first time around. Maybe 10 sit down the second time, then 5, then 2, then one, then one again until only one person is left standing. This person has predicted correctly the flip of the coin perhaps five or six times in a row. It is even within the realm of statistical probability that a person could predict the coin toss correctly ten or twelve times in a row.

What if you start with 400 hundred or 4000 or even 40,000 people? It will take more flips of the coin, but you will still end up with one person repeatedly making correct predictions. Is that because this person is more intelligent than the rest of the group or because she has a special gift that makes her unusually prescient? I think it is called "a string of lucky guesses."

The odds each time of calling the next toss correctly are exactly 50/50. This is not a reflection of analysis, insights, or psychic ability; it is strictly an application of the theory of large numbers. Any bell curve shows that there will be some incidence of unusual repetition. This is the basic flaw in the thinking of people who believe that they can move into and out of the market before there are big price movements. So many people are doing it that some are bound to be "right." But that only means that luck is at work, and luck inevitably runs out.

In recent years, we have seen a new kind of financial dysfunction in people who have gotten involved in what we call *Internet frontrunning*. This scam is perpetrated by con artists who single out a small company's lightly traded penny stock (i.e., stock priced under $1 a share). They buy a relatively large position in the stock, perhaps 10,000 shares for an average of 10 cents each, timing their purchases to force up the price. Then the perpetrators circulate e-mails, start blogs, and put posts on Internet discussion forums, touting the stock, how fast it is rising, and what tremendous prospects it has. As word spreads and more and more suckers buy into the false rumor, the price of the stock multiplies exponentially. Once the price rises to a high level, such as $10 a share, the scam artists sell their shares, thus turning $1,000 into $100,000 in a matter of weeks.

We started looking into this phenomenon and were discouraged to discover that not only was this a new dysfunction-arousing mechanism, but no laws are on the books to protect the public against it. Currently, there is no regulation of the Internet that requires a person's motivation be disclosed when he touts a hot stock. It was actually Internet postings that fueled much of the dot.com craze. Chat-site postings led to artificial demand, driving up prices. Someone would pick a penny stock and through positive hype run the price from $1 to $6, $8, or $10, then sell his shares to the last suckers who jumped on the bandwagon.

The February 25, 2001, edition of the *New York Times* carried a cover story in the magazine section about a 15-year-old boy whom the SEC targeted for market manipulation on the Internet. The author of the article, Michael Lewis, points out that the young man was not doing anything different than is done every day by the so-called market analysts who are employed by the world's largest Wall Street firms.

Market analysts employed by the major brokerage houses are paid to hype the companies whose stock offerings they handle and to steer lucrative underwriting work from the companies they hype to other departments at their firms. Their "buy" recommendations generally outnumber "sell" recommendations by a margin of 10 to 1. Little wonder that the analysts' compensation is partly determined by their effectiveness. What is incredible is that they get away with trading on their own account, buying and selling the very stocks they're touting before they make their analysis, in order to profit on the expected investor reaction.

It is technically illegal for stockbrokers to buy before their buy recommendations are printed or to sell their own shares while recommending that the public continue to buy. They are infrequently caught and then only given a slap on the wrist. This folly is well documented in the media and well known to experienced investors. Nonetheless, these supposed experts are still quoted, and their thoughts are still published and relied on by millions of naive investors who are convinced that somebody out there knows which is the next best stock to buy.

In May 2002, several brokerage houses copped a plea with the securities commissioner in New York. The settlement, however, only skims the surface of this outrageous conflict of interest. Brokerage companies are still not required to spin off their analysts so they are independent of the underwriting house; spinning off would mean setting up a separate or subsidiary company within the brokerage house. While the analysts are not specifically directed to enhance the ratings for stocks the brokerage is underwriting, they are still ultimately employed by the brokerage (and so, presumably, are sensitive to their employer's interests). Virtually all the stock brokerage companies have been fined for pressuring and/or offering incentives for their brokers to sell proprietary funds that the brokerage house sponsors. Sometimes quotas have been used, or a higher commission paid on these in-house funds, or contests are sponsored to treat their "top producers" to lavish trips to Hawaii or other destination resorts.

Morningstar, an independent mutual fund research company, recently released the "Study of the Decade," which found that the funds that brokers recommended underperformed the funds that individuals chose on their own, without even taking into account commissions. It is stunning, but not surprising, that advisors who claim to be working for their clients are so influenced by their one-sided training and self-interest that they are perfectly content with giving biased advice.

This isn't all the misinformation that plagues the financial functioning of people in all walks of life. Every few years we hear from the doom-and-gloom genre of authors, who forecast that economies will be devastated by energy shortages, nuclear war, and monetary collapse, or that a Great Depression is waiting just around the corner. Even the mainstream writers offer highly conflicting advice. Authors Joe Dominguez and Vicki Robin counsel you to put all your money into government bonds. Peter Lynch, by contrast, who gained such a sterling reputation running the Fidelity Magellan fund, wrote an article explaining why 100% of your investments should be in stocks.

> **The good news here is that you almost certainly have much more control over your financial fitness than you realize.**

The good news here is that you almost certainly have much more control over your financial fitness than you realize—in much the same way that people who commit to living a healthy lifestyle can suddenly discover that they enjoy better health than they imagined possible. These are the two simple keys: (1) knowing the actions that enable you to be functional financially, and (2) sticking to them regardless of outside media blather. Now let's look at how to exert that control over your financial life.

Your Own Road Map to Financial Freedom

> ❝ Money is coined liberty. ❞
> —FYODOR DOSTOYEVSKY

So how do you exercise control in your financial life? How do you start to develop financial fitness? At the heart of any financial plan are your goals. We use two exercises in our practice. The first helps you identify your goals and make sure they are congruent with your values. Then we lead you through a visualization exercise to anchor those goals. By using these techniques, we also avoid projecting our own goals onto our clients.

GOAL SETTING AND VALUES

You would think that goal setting would be at the top of our agenda, but in our offices we actually schedule it as one of the later appointments during a client's first year with us. Why? Because we must first gather enough information from earlier meetings to assess and put numbers to your goals. We do not encourage you to dream impossible dreams. Goals without numbers are fantasies. Our aim is to uncover what really matters to you—what it is that truly defines success for you. First we must determine what your values are.

Understanding Your Values

Study the below list of commonly held values. Now assume you have to give up ten of these values. Which would they be? Drop them out by putting an "X" in the left-hand column. Now rank-order the remaining five value preferences, from highest (1) to lowest (5). Place your ranking in the left-hand column. (Note that you may also add other values if you like, but you must end with only your top five values.) Once you've clarified your values, you can more easily determine your financial goals.

RANK	GOAL	DESCRIPTION
_____	**ACHIEVEMENT:**	To accomplish something important in life; be involved in significant activities; succeed at what I am doing.
_____	**ADVENTURE:**	To experience variety and excitement and be able to respond to challenging opportunities.
_____	**AESTHETICS:**	To be able to appreciate and enjoy beauty for beauty's sake; to be artistically creative.
_____	**AUTHORITY/POWER:**	To be a key decision maker, directing priorities, the activities of other people, and/or allocation and use of general resources.
_____	**AUTONOMY:**	To be independent, have freedom, and be able to live where I want to live and do what I want to do.
_____	**HEALTH:**	To be physically, mentally, and emotionally well; to feel energetic and maintain a sense of well-being.
_____	**INTEGRITY:**	To be honest and straightforward, just and fair.

EXERCISE 6.1

Understanding Your Values, *continued*

RANK	GOAL	DESCRIPTION
____	**INTIMACY/FRIENDSHIP/ LOVE:**	To have close personal relationships, experience affection, and share life with family and friends.
____	**PLEASURE:**	To experience enjoyment and personal satisfaction from the activities in which I participate.
____	**RECOGNITION:**	To be seen as successful; receive acknowledgment for achievements.
____	**SECURITY:**	To feel stable and comfortable with few changes or anxieties in my life.
____	**SERVICE:**	To contribute to the quality of life for other people and to be involved in improving society or the world.
____	**SPIRITUAL GROWTH:**	To have communication or harmony with the infinite source of life.
____	**WEALTH:**	To acquire an abundance of money and/or personal possessions; to be financially independent.
____	**WISDOM:**	To have insight, to be able to pursue new knowledge, have clear judgment, and be able to use common sense in life situations.
____	_____**(SPECIFY):**	To_____
____	_____**(SPECIFY):**	To_____

Note: Our thanks to Kathleen Rehl, PhD, CFP, for her kind permission to use this exercise.

This may be the first time you have actually looked at your values and consciously chosen to make financial decisions congruent with them. Exercise 6.1, "Understanding Your Values," shows a sampling of 15 key values people typically hold dear.

Once you define your goals, we can help strategize and prioritize what needs to be done to realize those goals—however they are defined—and to set a course for achieving them as time goes on.

Interestingly, the top goal of our clients is never to accumulate as large a pile of money as possible before dying. Most of you want to enjoy life with financial peace of mind rather than put all your efforts into making money. Our job is to help you structure your finances so you can have the kind of life you want.

I don't believe it is appropriate for a personal financial advisor to impose or assume values for any particular client. For example, many of my clients strongly believe in supporting their church and choose to tithe. Others make large donations to other philanthropic organizations such as the local symphony or the Humane Society. If the amount they're donating conflicts with their goals, however, I do point out that it will not be possible to both make those donations and reach their financial goals. The choice, however, is up to them.

The specific goal-setting process we use varies according to the client's stage in the Financial Life Cycle (see Chapter 7). People who are in the accumulation stages and have not yet retired receive the most benefit from goal-setting and visualization exercises. Those nearing the end of their careers may require retirement planning to project needs and means. Finally, people who have acquired more money than they can spend in their lifetimes need estate planning and gifting strategies.

We use a values identification exercise, available to the clients of all our Cambridge offices via our Web site. This exercise allows people to rate, on a scale from 1 (low) to 5 (high), the importance they attach to many commonly expressed goals. They can also specify and rank personal goals not included on the list. Once all goals are ranked, clients choose among the goals ranked the highest. We then compare the results of this forced-choice exercise to the original rankings. This is the first step in clarifying goals and identifying incongruence among stated goals, such as whether or not both partners rank paying for their children's college among their top five choices. Spouses or partners go through the exercise individually, so we can recognize and address differences in focus that could get in the way of realizing their goals. The exercise report can be printed and e-mailed to the client and the financial advisor. You can find the quiz at www.CambridgeAdvisors.com (Just click on the "Goals and Values Inventory"). Your spouse or partner should take the quiz at the same time, but do not look at each other's answers until you are done. The quiz will be computer-scored, and the results e-mailed back to you at no charge.

Most fee-only personal financial advisors help clients to identify their goals and values in a similar way. You can do this yourself by making a list of your priorities (such as early retirement, paying for your children's education, buying a new home, and so forth) and ranking them in order of importance. Then compare how closely your values align with your partner's values.

After reviewing the goals identified during the goal-setting exercise, we assess feasibility based on current resources and financial behaviors. Then we address the compatibility or incongruence of a couple's goals and values. We also provide appropriate education and then work to develop strategies and realistic time lines.

The goal-setting appointment starts out with a series of questions designed to identify and confirm symptoms of financial dysfunction. Here are some sample questions:

- What is your earliest memory of money?
- How did your parents handle money?
- If you did everything right, got your share of lucky breaks, and didn't make any major mistakes, how would you see your life in 5 years?
- How much would you be making?
- What would your net worth be?

One of the symptoms I see very frequently at this point is a poverty mentality: Clients accept externally imposed limitations on their financial success. Low expectations tend to become ceilings, and we tend to do those things that will raise us to the level of our ceilings—and not beyond.

> **Your goals must be realistic and congruent with your values if they are really to serve you.**

For instance, if you expect your income to double in 5 years, you will do things differently than someone who doesn't. You will start doing what's required to make that happen, such as taking a different job or getting an advanced degree, as opposed to expecting your income to rise only 3% a year.

You may, however, require a reality check. If you expect your income to quadruple within 5 years, and you don't intend to accomplish that by robbing banks or dealing drugs, what is the required price you have to pay to make that happen? It might be possible if you abandon your family and work 16- to 18-hour days, but is this the price you want to pay? Is this the life you want? Again, your goals must be realistic and congruent with your values if they are really to serve you.

VISUALIZATION EXERCISE

The second part of the goal-setting appointment is the visualization exercise. Seventy-five percent of the clients I work with are able to do this exercise and derive great value from it. I suggest that my clients close their eyes and relax. Then I lead them though a guided imagery process. After reading this scenario, try this yourself:

Assume that it is 5 years from now. You've done everything right. You didn't make any mistakes. You got your share of lucky breaks. These past 5 years have been great, each year better than the last. You've achieved all the things you wanted. You reached each one of your goals, and it's now 20XX (5 years from now).

This year is a terrific year for you. It's literally the best year of your life. Think through to the best day of that whole year. You get up in the morning and you feel great. You are healthy and you like the way you look. You have a lot of energy and you're looking forward to the day.

Today you can do all the things you really enjoy and get a lot of satisfaction from. You laugh a lot. It's one peak experience after another all day long. At night you go to bed and you run this day through your mind, remembering each experience from morning to night as if it were a movie.

Now rewind the movie to the most significant activity you did on this day, or just the very first one that comes to mind. Stop the movie as if doing a freeze frame, and focus on this activity. Now you have a still-life picture in your mind with you in the picture. Tell me what you see.

What I have found most revealing in 35 years of using this exercise with clients is that I have never had people describe flying off somewhere in their new Lear jet or sitting in a bank vault counting their bars of gold. The peak moments described are almost always simple things, dealing more with relationships than with acquisitions.

Whether indoors or outdoors, whether alone, with family, or with friends, or completely away from home, this picture represents the best of the best, your dream

> **The peak moments described are almost always simple things, dealing more with relationships than with acquisitions.**

come true. After you get everything you want, when it comes to the best moment of the best day of the best year of your life, the vision is where it leads. This visualization exercise can truly be eye-opening in its simplicity.

Next try adding more detail to the picture: *What day of the week is it? What time of day? What time of year? What are you hearing? What are you wearing? Who is with you? Are you sitting or standing?* Details provide many images that can give you insight into what you really want.

> **Usually clients who follow through with the anchoring exercise find themselves exactly in the scene they envisioned sooner than 5 years.**

Recently, a couple who had outgrown their home discussed the reasons they couldn't find a new home. They knew their children needed more room. The husband (who is a househusband) stressed how important a separate garage was for him to work on his race car. They could never find a house where he could work on his car. When we set time lines, however, he said he wanted to be out of racing within 5 years. In the visualization exercise he was standing in front of their new home with his wife, and there was no separate garage in the picture!

This process helped him realize that his self-esteem was actually based on being a full-time father. The race car was an obsolete prop that defined his old values. Within a week after that appointment, they made an offer on a home with a huge yard for their kids to play in.

It is usually helpful and fun for clients to follow up their visualization with an anchoring exercise. I ask them to pick a specific, consistent time each day for the next 21 days. During that few minutes, they again visualize that freeze-frame picture and add one more detail to it. They note in a journal their original picture, along with each added detail.

Once a week, they share the new details they've added with someone they've chosen as their visualization partner. They talk about what meaning the partner attributes to the added details; for example, if someone adds a suitcase to the picture, this could imply a desire to travel. At the end of the 21-day period, each gives the other a small, inexpensive gift of something in their vision. This symbolizes support and appreciation for one another's vision.

Then they keep their gift in plain sight—on their desk, dresser, or dashboard—where they will see it every day. They are reminded every day of what is really important in their lives. It represents the best that life can be for them. Usually clients who follow through with the anchoring exercise find themselves exactly in the scene they envisioned sooner than 5 years.

You can find a wealth of information between the lines of what you say in this exercise. Some aspects of the visualization are highly significant from a psychological standpoint; others less so. But what I consistently see between the lines is a search to feel economically secure and enjoy financial peace of mind.

The last comment I make in the goal-setting appointment is this: "Now our job is to structure your finances so you can achieve your vision."

The Financial Life Cycle: Benchmark Yourself

> " Money is better than
> poverty, if only for
> financial reasons. "
> —WOODY ALLEN

Not having benchmarks or standards to help you measure your progress contributes to financial dysfunction. Most people simply don't know how they measure up. They can only compare themselves to how they perceive others are doing based on purely external factors—the size of their house, the number and makes and ages of their cars, the frequency and destination of vacations—but these external factors reflect values and priorities, not necessarily financial well-being.

Almost all of us know someone older than we are who is struggling because of poor or neglected financial planning. Our society offers many examples of rock stars, movie stars, and sports stars who made a lot of money but didn't know what to do with it and ended up with nothing. They may have received bad advice or were simply ripped off by a supposedly trusted advisor.

In the first four chapters, you learned about financial dysfunction, your own financial personality, and some common symptoms of financial dysfunction. In Chapters 5 and 6 we discussed how an exogenous paradigm perpetuates financial dysfunction and how empowering it can be to shift to an endogenous one. In this chapter, you will complete your self-assessment by recognizing where you stand in your financial life.

Each stage of our financial life brings new challenges, confronts us with new issues, and requires new skills. As we'll see in a moment, your financial fitness regimen will be very different if you are just starting out your working life than it will be if you are newly retired.

> **Each stage of our financial life brings new challenges, confronts us with new issues, and requires new skills.**

I developed the Financial Life Cycle as a core part of my system to assess appropriate strategies for clients, and it's the starting point for asset allocation. We break the life cycle into stages that represent the natural progression in your personal financial development.

This is not to say that all financial progression is linear. In real life, the return on your investments may be turbocharged in prosperous times and it may slow to a crawl at other times. Death of a loved one, divorce, illness, disability, unemployment—the endogenous (internal) factors we have been discussing—can greatly affect your personal financial progression.

What I have seen repeatedly in my own practice is the need to complete the strategic fundamentals of each stage in the Financial Life Cycle before you can move on to the next one. So as you read these next chapters, remember that it is the specific factors characterizing each stage that matter, not the age ranges listed for each stage. Don't start thinking that you will never achieve financial fitness if you are not in the financial stage of your life that others reach at an earlier age. By the same token, beware of gloating if you are in a more advanced stage for your age, because often people who are more advanced at one stage end up falling behind later on. As it has been wisely stated, "Pride cometh before the fall."

CAPITALISM: UNDERSTANDING HOW THE GAME IS PLAYED

Understanding how capitalism works helps set the foundation for the concepts I discuss here and in Chapter 8. But beyond understanding the concepts, it will help you to progress through each stage and realize your goals of financial freedom and peace of mind. I find that many clients come to our doors because they are feeling stuck in a stage. Frequently, they are stuck because they do not grasp the concept of what it is to be financially independent and what it will take to get there.

First consider the three basic ways to obtain money. The first is by *affiliation:* You may marry into it, inherit it, or you may simply be given it. It's common to think that affiliation is the easy way to wealth, but my experience with thousands of clients tells me that this notion is a fallacy. In my experience, money acquired this way rarely lasts because the recipient never learned the basic concept of how to invest. You hear it expressed best in this old saying: "A fool and his money are soon parted." My clients are not fools, but their lack of knowledge— made worse by the misinformation that comes at them from every direction—can be debilitating.

The second way to obtain money is to earn it by the sweat of your brow. Although this is honorable, most people yearn to get to a point in their life where they can do what they want to do, what is self-actualizing for them, without having to worry about how much money they make. We like to say that one key financial goal is to make work optional—to attain financial freedom.

This brings us to the third way to make money, which is what financial freedom is all about. That is, *to let your money make money for you*, which requires regular saving and diligent investing. At some point in life, you will make yourself financially independent. How soon or late in life you reach that point largely depends on when you start saving and how much you save, as well as how well you invest your capital.

This is how capitalism works. When you produce more than you consume, you create a surplus which is your investment capital. That capital is saved and aggregated with the capital of others. We save this capital in banks, which then lend it to companies, or we buy stock that provides working capital for companies, or we invest it in real estate. Your invested capital grows and compounds over the years, as your past investment earnings now generate additional investment earnings on top of the money you are saving.

The goal is eventually to be able to live off the money your money makes, rather than the sweat of your brow. Then you are a winner: You not only have financial freedom, you are free to become, do, and have whatever you want!

That's how wealth is created—the capital we save is used to build plants, buy equipment, and develop things that make all of us richer. When a capitalistic society is working as designed, everyone is producing more than they consume. Then the amount produced by the society grows at an increasingly compounded rate. At this point, it is no longer an issue of how to divvy up the pie so it's even; rather, the social objective is to make sure the pie gets bigger and bigger so everyone can have a larger share in it.

As we go through the Financial Life Cycle, remember that the goal at each stage is eventually to have your money do the hard work. That is, your money earns the money you need in order to live a fulfilling life.

The Financial Life Cycle has four parts: the formative years, the accumulation years, the conservation years, and the largess years. Each part of the cycle is divided into two or more stages, discussed in detail here.

> The goal is eventually to be able to live off the money your money makes, rather than the sweat of your brow.

THE FORMATIVE YEARS

Three stages make up the formative years— early childhood, middle childhood and the teen years (see Table 7.1, "The Three Stages of the Formative Years"). Why are these critical stages in developing a person's financial fitness? Because the key to preventing financial dysfunction in the future is to improve how we educate our children about money during their formative years.

The Three Stages of the Formative Years

Stage	Early Childhood	Middle Childhood	Teen Years
Age	0–5	6–12	13–19
Financial Criteria	Learns the concept of value	Receives an allowance	Earns own money
Net Worth	N/A	N/A	N/A
Strategy	• Don't eat the money • Avoid waste	Learns basic concepts: • Accumulation • Money can be exchanged for things • Relative value	• Budgeting • Earned income • Money makes money
Asset Allocation	N/A	N/A	N/A

TABLE 7.1

Early Childhood

From birth to about 5 years old, children often test the world by trying to taste it. The first critical lesson about money we must teach our children, then, is "Don't eat the money!"

Eating money is neither a sound financial strategy nor a healthy habit. But often the biggest mistake parents make in this first stage is to let their kids eat the money! Maybe not literally (although many parents have experienced their child swallowing some change or slobbering all over a dollar bill or two), but eating the money is a metaphor for not respecting what we have.

Waste is a form of "eating the money." Kids must learn how to pour ketchup so half the bottle doesn't come out. Contrary to the TV commercials, they should learn that just a pea-size quantity of toothpaste does the job; covering the length of the toothbrush is wasteful. "Don't eat the money!" is teaching our children that waste is both uneconomical and environmentally unfriendly.

One of the best ways to cut waste is the law of halves: Keep cutting whatever you are using in half until it doesn't work anymore. For example, most people use too much shampoo when they wash their hair. Cut the amount you are using in half and see how that works. If your hair gets clean, great! Then cut it in half again. Now it's not enough? Then add a little back until you find the right amount. Most children are not taught how to determine the correct amount to use—whether it's ketchup, toothpaste, or shampoo.

Freedom from financial dysfunction—financial independence—is all about knowing how much is enough. It's not just a money issue. Nor is it a matter of deprivation. It's about living life to its fullest and getting the most value out of the resources you can access.

If focusing on how much toothpaste you use seems extreme, consider this. In our own (less than scientifically controlled) test, a 4.4 oz, $3.33 tube of toothpaste applied to a child-size toothbrush in the quantity shown on TV commercials provided 80 uses—enough for 40 days, provided it doesn't continually fall off the brush into the sink! At that rate, your child would use nine tubes of toothpaste per year, at an average monthly cost of $2.50.

If that usage were cut in half, the child would save $1.25 per month. If that $1.25 per month were saved over your child's life expectancy—say from age 1 to age 80—and invested at an average 10% yearly rate of return—the total would come to $391,413!

If the usage were cut in half again (which would still provide the required dental results), the savings over a lifetime would approach $590,000! Now multiply that times the number of mundane condiments and

> **Freedom from financial dysfunction—financial independence—is all about knowing how much is enough.**

personal care items we use every day. Even if your child did not leave the money invested to compound for 80 years, what else could be done with that money besides spitting it down the drain? Go to a better college? Enjoy the opera? Achieve financial independence sooner?

The point is not to start yelling at your child about amounts of toothpaste. It is fun to teach your children these principles from a very early age, like a game. Discover the minimum amount needed to get the required results. "Waste not, want not" is more of a truth than most of us realize!

Middle Childhood

From age 6 to about age 12, children start learning about the relative value of money. For example, they learn that dimes are worth more than nickels even though they are smaller and that a quarter buys more than a dime. During this stage we form our basic belief systems about money.

Typically, kids at this time start collecting things—seashells, butterflies, and so on. We can promote and encourage their natural inclinations and urges to explore by teaching them to accumulate money.

Most clients who are good savers now started as children with a piggy bank on their dresser. It was a standard fixture in the bedroom. Kids like to save things. This makes middle childhood an opportune moment to give children a vehicle to start accumulating money and to teach them how to save effectively.

> We need to teach kids the difference between money they can spend now versus these other kinds of money:
>
> 1. Money set aside to give away (whether to friends, family, houses of worship, or charities)
> 2. Money they save up to buy something substantial later on (like a bike)
> 3. Money saved permanently for investment capital.

In my 35+ years of tending to a variety of financial maladies, I've learned that we communicate to our children many of our own values simply by the way we handle money. Children learn money sense primarily by imitation. Let's start with money they get to spend now, which in most families means an allowance.

> **We communicate to our children many of our own values simply by how we handle money.**

Sometimes we give our children mixed messages. One client of mine who was a single parent often told her children, "The most important thing when you have money is to pay your bills first!" This was a backhanded slap at her ex-husband, who was always late with the child support. One day I asked her about the allowances she paid her children. She replied that she usually gave them $2 a week, when she remembered, but at that point she was several weeks behind. I suggested that she consider the mixed message her children might be getting from the disconnect between her admonitions and her behavior.

Saving to Give

Teaching about money we give to others communicates the values of generosity and gratitude. We have an obligation that goes beyond our families and ourselves to the communities we live in—to support them and share the affluence we have with people who are less fortunate.

We want our children to learn that a lot of the enjoyment and value we get out of material things comes from being grateful for our good fortune and expressing that gratitude. We teach them that we can never enjoy something fully if we don't express the gratitude for having it, for it is the expression of gratitude that completes the cycle.

One of my most vivid memories of Christmas as a child involves this dynamic relationship of the expression of gratitude. We lived in southern Arizona on the Mexican border. Every Christmas, my dad would load up the back of the station wagon with bags of fruit and little presents—but mostly fruit and food. We would drive across the border and give these to the many poor families living there in mud huts.

The first time we did this I was mortified. To me, receiving an orange for Christmas seemed like a punishment—as if, perhaps, you'd been a bad kid. The only thing worse was to receive underwear! But when I saw how grateful these kids were for what I took for granted, it put my life in perspective.

Saving to Buy Things Later

By saving up for things we want, we teach children the value of delayed gratification. A common dysfunction that wreaks havoc on financial freedom is this approach: "If I want something, I should buy it right now and put it on my credit card." Children need to learn to identify what they want, set savings goals, save the money, and then go and buy it when (and if) they have reached their goal.

Not only will they appreciate the item more, it will also be more meaningful. They will also discover that what seemed so important last week isn't so important today. In later life, they will understand that things cost less if saved for and bought with cash, rather than paying credit card interest. If kids aren't taught this lesson at this stage, it is a very difficult practice to learn later in life.

Investment

Saving for investment is a concept beyond the capacity of most children between 6 and 12 to grasp fully. Those who are more mature or precocious will benefit from opening a bank savings or checking account, or buying stock, but this concept forms the fundamental lessons of the next stage.

As children mature, it is appropriate to increase their allowance. Concomitant with the increase should be additional financial responsibilities. For example, at around age 8 or 10, children's allowances might be increased to cover the cost of lunch money. From then on, children are responsible to set aside money for their lunch themselves. Later on, when they are in their early teens, an increase may include an amount appropriate for them to spend on clothes so they can buy their own wardrobe.

These techniques teach children that mishandling money has

consequences, and parents must also enforce those consequences. If children squander their lunch money, they must make their own lunch and bring it to school until they receive their next allowance!

The Teen Years

From ages 13 to 19, children begin to learn how money is earned: Work is rewarded with money, money can be made by buying something and then reselling it at a profit, and money saved earns interest. The idea that money can make money with investments is often a hard lesson to learn, because children have to save money first to get started investing.

The verb "to save" in the English language is very ambiguous. Often I ask clients if they save money regularly and they smile and assure me that they do. So why don't they have any investments? Oh, they reply, because we end up spending it. Saving up money to spend later doesn't count as investing!

Teenagers need to learn that the name of the game is capitalism. First, all people in society must create value for others, for which they are then paid. Then they must produce more than they consume (in other words, live within their means). This enables them to create a surplus. As that surplus accumulates over time, it can be invested. Their investments enable our society to expand and create jobs and prosperity, and the investments appreciate. Eventually, your children will have enough invested so that they won't have to work anymore: They can live off the money their money makes.

> **Teenagers need to learn that the name of the game is capitalism.**

Teenagers generally understand the advantage of being able eventually to live off the money their capital generates rather than off the sweat of their brow. If we show them how to earn money and then how to invest it, they will appreciate the lesson later in life.

Investing must start by setting aside money with the sole purpose of investing it. It is not for spending now, not for spending later, not for giving away. It is saved so the money can make money. Moreover, money saved at an early age becomes much more valuable than money saved later in life because of what I call the *magic of compounding*.

Most of the parents I have talked to in my practice acknowledge that the most important lesson they did *not* get from their parents, and so could not pass on to their children, was the basic concept of investments. Let's begin by understanding the principle of compounding.

Figure 7.1 illustrates what could happen if your child begins as a teenager to save money for investment. In this example we have Mary, who is 15 years old. Each year for the next 5 years she saves $3,000 from her earnings from her part-time job and from monetary gifts and

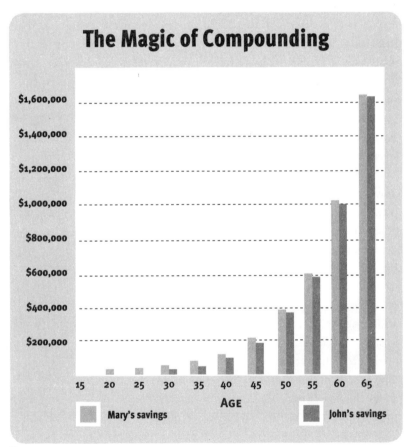

FIGURE 7.1

puts it in an investment with a 10% return. At the age of 20 (after 5 years), she never saves another dime for investments, but simply allows her savings ($15,000) and accumulated earnings to continue to grow at a 10% compounded rate.

Her twin brother John, however, waits until after college (age 25) to begin saving for investment. He saves $3,000 every year of his working life—until age 65 (40 years), and also invests it at a 10% compounded rate of return.

At age 65, Mary, who saved for only 5 years, will have accumulated $1,468,512. John, who saved for 40 years, will have only $1,463,555! Therefore, although Mary had only put $15,000 of her savings into investments, she amassed more capital than John, who had invested $120,000! Clearly, the key to financial freedom is to learn to begin investing at an early age because it allows for more compounding. Even if you haven't yet started, remember that you are younger now than you ever will be again—so start saving and investing now!

Just think of how much further ahead your children will be if they start an investment program in their teens! If they don't, they will spend the rest of their life trying to catch up.

Two things happen that tend to trip teens up during this stage. The first is that they can get sidetracked with the idea of earning their own way. Because they are not sophisticated enough to understand the cost of supporting themselves, they may think they can just get a job working at the local McDonald's and make enough money to buy a car or take a trip. Teenagers often get the message that they can spend the money they earn on the impulse of the moment and their parents will continue paying for the fundamentals of life. Reality is the best antidote to this particular financial dysfunction, but as parents we tend to shield our children from these harsh facts. Teenagers need clear instruction and direction to establish the habit of regular saving for long-term investment.

If your teens are only responsible for the extras, they will not learn the cost of the basics. Your teens need enough money to make mistakes and experience the consequences of having made those mistakes. So if you give your teens a $300 budget to buy school clothes, they need to understand (or learn) that if they decide to buy a $300 leather jacket, that's it. Everything else they wear comes from last year's wardrobe, or they will have to dip into their other disposable income (say, gifts from grandparents) and shop at secondhand stores. If they buy the $300 leather jacket and then you still come through with the money for them to buy other clothes, they will have missed a very valuable lesson.

> **Your teens need enough money to make mistakes and experience the consequences of having made those mistakes.**

For many parents, setting these boundaries is not easy. Recognizing our own financial dysfunctions and how they influence our children can be painful work. But there's clear value in learning these lessons while the cost is still minimal. It is more painful to watch an adult child lose his or her home or declare bankruptcy. I once had clients who were still bailing their grown children out of debt when their children were in their thirties and forties. Finally, my clients used up all their nonretirement funds and reached the point in life where they could no longer work. I insisted that they put their foot down and make their kids pay their own way. It was tough to maintain a hard line—especially when the kids appealed for money to pay for the grandchildren's expenses—but eventually their kids were forced to get credit counseling and reduce their standard of living significantly. Of course, they had diminished their parents' standard of living as well for the rest of their lives.

Here's the second thing that trips teens up: Although they learn that they can work and earn money, they may fail to learn that what they earn is fundamentally determined by the value they add. Teen entrepreneurs tend to learn this lesson sooner and more easily because the relationship is clear and direct: If you get results, you are paid. If there are no results, there's no pay. For teens who work for someone else, the connection between working and adding value can get quite murky: They may not actually be creating value at all, if they are given busywork or are performing duties that have outlived their usefulness. Teaching teens to focus on creating value in the work they do—by showing up on time, answering the phone within three rings, accurately balancing the cash register—will help them to maximize their effectiveness and value their contributions correctly throughout their working lives.

THE ACCUMULATION YEARS

Three stages also make up the next phase of the Financial Life Cycle, the accumulation years. This stage includes building the foundation, early accumulation, and rapid accumulation (see Table 7.2).

The Accumulation Stages of the Financial Life Cycle

Stage	Building the Foundation	Early Accumulation	Rapid Accumulation
Age	20–30	30–40	40–50
Financial Criteria	Becomes self-supporting	Net worth more than annual income	Investment earnings exceed savings
Net Worth	Less than annual income	1–3 times annual income	3–7 times annual income
Strategy	Five fundamentals of fiscal fitness	Diversify into stocks and bonds	Increase tax efficiency and risk
Asset Allocation	75% interest-earning/ 25% equities	50% interest-earning/ 50% equities	40% interest-earning/ 60% equities

TABLE 7.2

Building the Foundation

We enter this stage when we start to be completely self-supporting, usually in our early twenties. Because of a changing world, parents and society alike generally do a poor job of providing basic financial education at the middle school, high school, and even college levels. As a result, I find my focus as a personal financial advisor at this foundation stage often is to help my clients acquire the basic knowledge and skill set to become savvy consumers.

> ### For most people, building the foundation stage requires a multitude of first-time decisions:
>
> - How do I evaluate competing job offers?
> - Should I contribute to my 401(k)? How much?
> - How do I choose between my 401(k) options?
> - Should I buy or lease a car? How much car can I afford?
> - What is my best financing option?
> - What about car insurance? What do I really need?
> - Do I need life insurance? Disability insurance?
> - Do I need a will?
> - Should I rent an apartment or buy a home?
> - If buying, how much home can I afford, and what do I look for in financing?
> - If renting, how do I evaluate a lease agreement?

Add in income taxes, marriage, and possibly children, and it's easy to see why so many people struggle at this stage.

The key to moving through this stage is to accomplish the five fundamentals of fiscal fitness. Let's look at each of these five fundamentals in greater detail.

The Five Fundamentals of Fiscal Fitness	**1.** Save at least 10% of annual income.
	2. Have sufficient liquidity.
	3. Fully fund pensions.
	4. Buy the right house for your budget.
	5. Pay off credit cards and consumer debt.

Save at Least 10% of Annual Income

As we discussed earlier, in our society you are expected to produce more than you consume. In other words, you are expected to live within your means. The difference between what you produce and what you consume—the surplus—is what you save as invested capital. You don't save it to spend it later—you save it to invest. Down the road, as that money is invested to earn more money, eventually you will be able to live off the money your money makes instead of by the sweat of your brow. That is capitalism. That is financial freedom. That is the goal of investment capital.

Saving for large expenditures, by contrast, involves deciding how much of each paycheck you will set aside for big-ticket items—furniture, a trip, home improvements, a car, and so on. You plan and save for these expenditures so you do not need to incur any debt when acquiring them. Generally speaking, you save for about a year before you spend the money allocated for these big-ticket items with this type of savings.

When I talk about saving 10% of annual income, I am talking about permanent savings—saving for investment capital. Sometimes during the foundation stage, people believe they don't make enough money to set any aside anything as savings. My many years of experience have demonstrated conclusively to me that the amount someone earns in no way correlates to the percentage of income he or she can save. I have clients who make $30,000 a year and save 10%, plus they tithe to their church. And I have clients who make $100,000 a year and are buried in credit card debt and neither save nor make donations at all.

Others who did not learn to delay gratification as children believe they can't afford to save because they have so many things they want to buy and do. Still other people with financial dysfunctions have so many things they have already bought and done (on credit) that they don't believe they can pay their bills and save money at the same time. If your goal is financial fitness and independence, it is vitally important to begin your permanent savings program as early as possible, so you can make the magic of compounding work for you.

Saving 10% of everything you make is "fundamental"—a lifetime recommendation. Saving 10% of your income consistently will enable you to live off the money your money makes in 25 to 35 years. After retirement, continuing to save 10% each year will offset inflation and ensure that you will never run out of money. If you are always saving 10% of your income, you are always living within your means! Failing to live within your means is the basic cause of virtually all financial problems. When people have severe debt problems or are facing bankruptcy, it is usually because they have not lived within their means.

> If you want the one secret to financial fitness, it would be this: Make the commitment now to save 10% of your income.

Excessive consumer debt is a clear signal that you are living beyond your means. Basically, you may be trying to be someone you are not by living a lifestyle you cannot afford. This results in a heavy psychological burden you carry around, compounded by guilt, shame, and fear. Spiritually, you are off-balance because your integrity is compromised.

If you want the one secret to financial fitness, it would be this: Make the commitment now to save 10% of your income. If you don't think you will get over feeling the pinch, just think about the reverse situation. Have you ever received a 10% raise? Didn't you feel rich? How long did that feeling last? I bet it lasted only 2 to 3 months. Then it felt like the money was never there. You incorporated it into your standard of living and it vanished.

> **Failing to live within your means is the basic cause of virtually all financial problems.**

It works the same way with saving. If you make $42,000 per year and start saving $350 a month to meet your 10% savings commitment, you will feel that pinch for a month or two. But after that, you will never notice it again for the *rest of your life!* You will have secured your financial future! Saving that amount over a period of 36 years at a market rate of return will enable you to accumulate $1 million—which is sufficient to enable you to continue saving 10%, pay income taxes, and still have enough left over to maintain your standard of living without having to earn a penny for the rest of your life.

What if you have a student loan at a 9% rate of interest? Or if you've made some mistakes in the past and you have a lot of credit card debt at 18%? Isn't it more important to pay off the debt first?

No. The reason you have so much debt is because you are so good at paying it off. The reason you have no savings is because you are not very good at saving. The only way to effect permanent change is to start saving while you pay off your debt. It may not seem rational—to be saving money that is earning only 3% when you are paying credit card interest of 18%—but it is psychologically significant.

I have seen this time and time again with my clients. Those who save 10% while paying off their debt continue saving and securing their financial future long after they are debt free. Those who pay off their debt without simultaneously saving may become debt free more quickly, but they do not replace their old negative habit with a new positive habit. They feel compelled to reward themselves for paying off their debt, usually by buying something that puts them right back into debt again.

See Exercise 7.1, "Your Current Savings," to get a picture of how much you currently save.

Have Sufficient Liquidity

After making the commitment to save 10% of their income, the next question most people ask is, "Where should I be investing these savings?" The first goal is to have adequate cash reserves.

Your Current Savings

Out of every (check one) Year _____ Month ___ Paycheck ___

you save $_____ out of $_____ in gross earnings.

Savings that count are permanent savings intended to fund your retirement. These could be saved in the categories listed here. Fill in the approximate amounts you are saving.

Pensions*: $_____

Cash for future investment: $_____

Mutual funds: $_____

Brokerage accounts: $_____

U.S. savings bonds: $_____

Life insurance or annuities: $_____

Now divide your savings by your earnings to figure out your percentage savings rate:

Savings $_____

_____ =_____ ×100 =_____%

Earnings $_____

*For example, 401(k), IRA, SEP, SIMPLE, and so on.

EXERCISE 7.1

Many financial pundits in the media say everyone should have cash reserves equal to 3 to 6 months of income. For most middle-income people, that is simply a pipe dream. According to that formula, someone earning $40,000 a year would need to have $10,000 to $20,000 in the bank in cash reserves.

With our clients, I use a different and more realistic approach. I recommend that those who are employed by someone else maintain a minimum balance in their checking or savings account of 10% of their annual income. For the person who earns

> **Sufficient liquidity is the foundation of your financial freedom.**

$40,000 a year, this means $4,000—a far more feasible goal. This money will earn interest and usually will enable you to get free checking and other free bank services. It will also cover about 2 months of your usual living expenses, so you will have adequate cash flow.

For the self-employed, the goal is 20%. Adequate liquidity carries additional benefits for those in business for themselves. Many self-employed people make the mistake of living out of the cash drawer. They lose control of their cash by doing this and also leave themselves vulnerable to theft. Not being able to balance the cash drawer enables employees to help themselves to the cash drawer too, because it's too hard to tell how much is missing. For the self-employed, the family unit is subject to periods of feast or famine, depending on short-term business cycles. Adequate liquidity ensures stability and peace of mind for the entire family, despite this challenge.

For those in retirement, adequate liquidity is key to enjoying the wealth they've earned. Because they are no longer earning money, many are unable to make the leap that allows them to enjoy their wealth. Often, they need to have permission to spend so they need to feel financially comfortable. Therefore, for those in retirement, my recommendation for base liquidity is 30% of annual income so a comfortable cash cushion is available to provide for cash flow. For retirees afflicted with deprivation anxiety, it may be appropriate to

Minimum Base Liquidity

If you are...	Then you should have...
Employed by someone else and earning a predictable income	10% of your annual income in cash savings
Self-employed, or in commissioned sales, or earning a fluctuating income	20% of your annual income in cash savings
Retired	30% of your annual income in cash savings
Facing layoff or unemployment	40% of your annual income in cash savings

TABLE 7.3

have even more liquidity (see Chapter 4). Finally, for those who are facing the prospect of becoming unemployed—perhaps preparing for a pending layoff—I recommend 40% (about 5 to 6 months of liquidity) to give them sufficient breathing room to find a new job. Table 7.3 summarizes how much you should keep as a minimum in your checking or savings account.

Once this cash reserve level is met, the next liquidity goal is emergency liquidity. *Emergency* does not mean the car breaks down, the roof starts leaking, or you need a new outfit for your high school reunion. We are talking about permanent savings. We define an emergency as any time your tax bracket drops, which often accompanies a substantial decrease in income. If you are disabled or unemployed for a protracted period, you may be in an emergency situation. This second level of liquidity helps protect you under those circumstances.

The amount saved as emergency liquidity should be twice the amount required for cash reserves. So if you are employed and earning $40,000 a year, and have $4,000 in the bank as cash reserves, the amount you require in emergency liquidity is $8,000. We recommend a higher level of emergency liquidity for individuals with high mortgage balances, as we discuss in Chapter 8.

Do not keep emergency liquidity in your checking or savings account. Instead, put this money in a retirement account (IRA, 401[k], etc.), money market fund, or in U.S. saving bonds. For some people, the biggest threat to liquidity is that money burns a hole in their pocket. If there is money in the bank, they have to spend it. Building emergency liquidity in pension funds or U.S. savings bonds can put this temptation out of reach, plus this practice enables you to build a much more tax-efficient portfolio.

There is a tax and/or interest rate consequence to withdrawing these funds. However, because you only use these funds in situations when your tax bracket drops, you will still come out ahead financially. As an example, let's say you are in the 28% federal tax bracket. Money you put into a traditional deductible IRA is tax deferred, so if you allocate $2,000, then $560 (i.e., 28% of $2,000) in taxes is deferred. You later experience a qualifying emergency and have to withdraw this money. You will have to pay a 10% penalty for early withdrawal and taxes on the money, but because you are now in a 15% tax bracket, the total of penalty and tax due is only $500 (i.e., a total of 25% of the $2,000 withdrawn). As you can see in Table 7.4, you are still $60 ahead.

Many people chafe at the idea of having this sum of money (cash reserves plus emergency liquidity) tied up in cash and cash equivalents. They want to be investing in the stock market now. They don't want to have a large sum of money earning low rates of interest. This strategy seems too conservative to them. Many people go 5, 10, or 20 years without ever needing to draw on the emergency liquidity that has been set aside. But even though you don't use it, it still has to there.

Sufficient liquidity is the foundation of your financial freedom. The depth and solidity of any foundation determines the strength and height of the structure that can be built on it. Any building constructed on a faulty or incomplete foundation will ultimately topple. You need to stay focused and patient as you complete and maintain your foundation.

Effective Withdrawal of Tax-Deferred Emergency Liquidity

	Pre-Emergency	Upon Emergency
Taxable Income/ (Tax Bracket)	$40,000 (28%)	$20,000 (15%)
IRA Contribution/Withdrawal	+$2,000	–$2,000
Taxes Deferred/Due	–$560	–$300
Penalty Due on Early Withdrawal	N/A	–$200 (10%)
Total Tax Benefit/Cost	–$560	–$500

TABLE 7.4

Sufficient liquidity and a solidly constructed financial foundation also serve as your bulwark against what I call the "triple whammy." At some point in life, almost everyone comes up against a triple whammy: three catastrophic events within a 6-month period. You lose your job, your spouse becomes disabled, and the stock market crashes. Your partner has a heart attack, you get laid off, and your house burns down. Your child becomes very ill, you take an unpaid family leave of absence to care for her, and your elderly parents become unable to care for themselves or pay for a caregiver. Decisions you make during the foundation years determine whether you will survive a triple whammy or become devastated financially.

Failure to maintain adequate liquidity creates a continuing danger that short-term cash flow interruptions will force you to cash in long-term investments at the wrong time. This is a costly mistake that some people make over and over again; as a result, they are never able to build an investment portfolio.

Fully Fund Pensions

As we discussed earlier, the employer-funded, defined-benefit pension plan has pretty much gone the way of the dinosaur. Personal contributory pensions that are portable (immediately vested so the employee keeps them when changing jobs) have replaced it. The government encourages these by giving special tax breaks to both employer and the employee. Employers like them because they save money—even with a matching program and administrative costs, the costs to an employer are far less than those of a defined-benefit plan. Employees like them because they are portable, provide direct tax savings, and let them decide which investments to make.

> **Virtually everyone should contribute to the tax-deferred pensions available to them.**

The basic advantage of all personal pensions (with the exception of nondeductible IRAs and Roth IRAs, discussed later) is that the contributions are tax deferred. This means that whatever money you put into the pension becomes a tax deduction now, and the tax otherwise due on that income is deferred until you take the money out. In addition, the earnings on your contributions also accrue on a tax-deferred basis.

Retirement plans through your employer are usually the easiest way to save money (and note that these savings count toward your 10% permanent savings). Your plan might be called a 401(k), a 403(b), or a tax-deferred savings plan. These are good places to save your money and are especially attractive when your employer has a matching program.

Self-funded pension opportunities have been expanded to the point where fully funding the pension options available may be almost impossible for many people. One stupid thing some people do is make extra payments on their mortgage when they could be putting that extra money in a pension account. Most companies have a 401(k) plan that allows employees to defer 15% of their earnings—up to a limit, which is increased every year or so. (At the time of this writing in

2006, the limit was $14,000 a year, so if you earned $60,000 a year, to fully fund your 401(k) you'd need to contribute $9,000, 15% of $60,000). Note that some employers match the first 3% to 6% you contribute. Some employers now offer Roth 401(k)s, but I don't recommend funding a Roth unless you are in a 15% tax bracket or lower. The tax savings generated by pension contributions when you are in a higher bracket are too substantial to pass up, and I have found that most people are able to convert pension money into Roths at a later date, when they are in a 15% bracket.

Many people now are also eligible to fund a deductible IRA or a Roth IRA. Most families will not be able to afford to fully fund all these pension options. But it is still critical to your financial independence to use all available pension options to your best advantage in order to maximize the benefits of saving money on a tax-deferred basis.

Virtually everyone should contribute to the tax-deferred pensions available to them. The only exception I can see is the very small percentage of people with negative taxable income, meaning they have more deductions on their tax return than they have income. In this case, a tax-deferred pension would actually be funded with money that is already completely nontaxable, creating a situation in which tax-free funds would be converted to taxable funds in the future when they're withdrawn. For example, if you have an annual income of $30,000, but your deductions in a particular year add up to $35,000 because of high medical bills, you would have a negative taxable income of $5,000. So you would not save any taxes by funding a 401(k), since you aren't paying any taxes. In such a case, however, it is wise to fund a Roth IRA. Roth contributions are not deductible, but when withdrawn for college expenses, a down payment on a first home, or disability, the funds are totally tax free and without penalty. The original contributions can be withdrawn at any time without tax or penalty.

Why do I think everyone else should contribute? Because no other investment can match the advantage of tax deferral. Think of it this way: Suppose you are in a 28% federal tax bracket and a 5% state tax bracket, for a combined tax bracket of 33%. For every $300 you contribute to your tax-deferred pension, $100 of taxes is deferred. To look at it another way, it only costs you $200 to contribute $300 to your pension. In effect, the government is contributing $1 for each $2 you contribute. If you are in a 15% tax bracket, the argument is somewhat less compelling—the government contributes $1 for every $4 you contribute—but it is still quite a good deal.

But wait. You do have to pay taxes on this money eventually, don't you? So is this really as good a deal as it seems? Keep these scenarios in mind about having to pay taxes on this later. First, it is entirely possible you will be in a lower tax bracket when you withdraw this money in an emergency or at retirement. If you are in a 28% tax bracket when you make the contributions and a 15% bracket when you make the withdrawals (upon retirement, for example), you will have received a substantial advantage of 13%.

Second, assume that your tax bracket does remain the same at retirement. As the graph in Figure 7.2 shows, the interest you will have earned in 7 to 12 years just on the taxes you originally deferred is sufficient to pay all the taxes ultimately due.

As you can see in Figure 7.2, if you were to invest $2,000 each year in a tax-deferred pension plan earning an annual 9% tax-deferred rate of return, you would have over $169,000 after 25 years. Contrast this with investing $1,400 of after-tax dollars in an investment earning 6% (after taxes) per year for a total return of only $76,810. Even after paying 33% taxes on the $169,000 at the end of the 25 years, you would be left with $113,000. This is almost 50% more than the non-tax-deferred account. The breakeven point comes between years 9 and 10, when the tax-deferred interest is equal to the tax you would have to pay on the money if it were withdrawn at that time (assuming a total tax rate of 33%). After you pass the breakeven point, the interest earned on the taxes deferred alone will cover the tax liability for early withdrawal.

Some people resist contributing to pensions because they believe they can't get to the money until they are old. Retirement is not the only reason you could withdraw money from your pension, IRA, or 401(k). Current tax law allows some penalty-free withdrawals for education, purchasing a home, or if you are disabled.

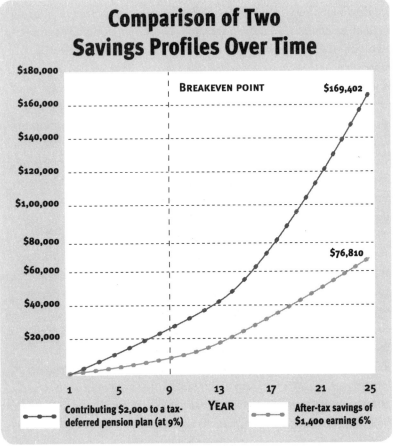

Comparison of Two Savings Profiles Over Time

BREAKEVEN POINT

$169,402

$76,810

YEAR

Contributing $2,000 to a tax-deferred pension plan (at 9%)

After-tax savings of $1,400 earning 6%

FIGURE 7.2

Remember how we defined an emergency as a drop in your tax bracket? Maybe you decide you want to stop work to travel the world or start your family. Maybe you experience a disability or an extended period of unemployment. In these cases, where a drop in tax bracket occurs, you could withdraw funds, pay the penalty, and still come out ahead. I have even recommended to clients that they withdraw funds from retirement accounts when they experience negative taxable income, even if they don't need the money. This is especially common for entrepreneurs and for people in the real estate business, who experience wide swings in their tax bracket.

How much should you contribute? If you are permitted to contribute 10% of income, I recommend that you do so. In certain situations involving highly compensated employees, it may not be possible to contribute 10%. If you are not permitted to contribute 10%, contribute as much as you are allowed. If you are allowed to contribute more than 10%, and you can afford to do so, contribute the maximum you are allowed. Certainly, if your employer provides a matching contribution, contribute at least up to the amount the employer is matching. Max out what your employer will match. However, if you are investing in your employer's stock in your 401(k) plan, or are receiving a matching contribution from your employer, make sure the total amount invested in company stock does not exceed 20% of your total equities.

Too often employees of a company underestimate the risk of their employer's stock. Since there are often several different ways that an employee can accumulate employer's stock, such as options, employee stock purchase plans, and 401(k) matches, it is easy to soon become overweighted in the stock. Failure to diversify out of your employer's stock is a serious, possibly disastrous, financial blunder. Too many financial aspects of your life, including your paycheck and your pension, are already dependent on the well-being of your company. If your portfolio also becomes vulnerable to your employer's failure, the risk becomes overwhelming. The employees of Enron learned this when their employer went bankrupt and employees whose investments were primarily in Enron stock were also forced into bankruptcy.

Remember that the second fundamental of fiscal fitness is adequate liquidity. In some situations, and depending on your tax bracket, you may need to save less than the maximum allowed in your pension so you can also be building your cash reserves. But here's the beauty of tax-deferred savings: You can use the money you save in taxes on your pension contribution toward building your liquidity.

In Exercise 7.2, "How Much Are You Saving in Pension Plans?," fill in your own information to see how much you are saving.

Buy the Right Value House for Your Financial Situation
For most middle-income people, buying a house is the best possible

How Much Are You Saving in Pension Plans?

Plan Type	Available to Me? (circle)		Amount Saved per Year	Percentage of Gross Income
Your IRAs	Y	N	$	%
Partner's IRAs	Y	N	$	%
Your workplace savings plans	Y	N	$	%
Partner's workplace savings plans	Y	N	$	%
Your self-employed plans	Y	N	$	%
Partner's self-employed plans	Y	N	$	%
Total			$	%

EXERCISE 7.2

investment. It doesn't make sense to consider buying mutual funds, stocks, or bonds if you don't have a house. Let's discuss several reasons why.

The first reason is the long-term leverage you receive when buying a house. *Leverage* is an important investment concept to understand. Let's say you buy a $200,000 house with a 20% down payment of $40,000. If your house appreciates 4% a year (the average historical appreciation for real estate), it will increase $8,000 per year. That appreciation represents a 20% return on your $40,000 investment and a tax-free return to boot! The first $500,000 ($250,000 if you're

> For most middle-income people, buying a house is the best possible investment.

Home Ownership Is Within Your Reach

	Per Year	Per Month
Total house payment for a $200,000 house financed with a $160,000 30-year fixed mortgage at 6% fixed interest	$15,000	$1250
Tax savings (25% federal tax bracket)	$3000	$250
House payment after tax savings	$12,000	$1000
Total rent payment	$11,400	$950
After-tax increase in housing costs	$600	$50

TABLE 7.5

single) gained from the sale of your primary residence is excluded from taxation. You can't get that kind of return on investment anywhere else with the low risk of home ownership.

The second reason is the way our tax system is structured. In effect, the government heavily subsidizes homeowners. It is a fundamental American value to own your own home, which is reflected in our tax system. The mortgage interest and property taxes you pay are tax deductible. As a result, virtually your entire house payment will be tax deductible because it takes over 21 years for the amount allocated to principal to exceed the amount allocated to interest on a conventional 30-year mortgage.

To illustrate, let's continue our example of a $200,000 home purchased with a $40,000 down payment, leaving a mortgage of $160,000 at 6% (see Table 7.5, "Home Ownership Is Within Your Reach"). Your monthly payment (principal and interest only) would be $959.28, based on a standard 30-year amortization table. Let's assume a total payment (taxes and insurance included) of $1250. You currently pay rent at $950 a month and immediately assume there is no way you can afford an additional $300 a month to buy a home. Let's look a little more closely at that assumption. Of that $1250 monthly payment, approximately $1000, which represents interest and taxes, will be tax deductible (in year one). That is a $12,000 tax deduction the first year, which in a 25% federal bracket yields a $3,000 tax savings. Spread that throughout the year, the monthly tax savings works out to $250, so it's actually costing you only an additional $50 per month to buy that house, not $300.

This calculation doesn't even begin to take into account the other tax benefits of home ownership. Under current tax law, realized gains of up to $250,000 (single) or $500,000 (married) are tax free! In other words, you buy that $200,000 house and live there at least 2 years, enjoying the tax benefits of your deductible mortgage interest and taxes. If you then decide to sell that house, you would not have to pay any capital gains tax (income tax levied on profits from sales of assets) on the sale unless the house sold for more than $450,000 (single) or $700,000 (married).

And here's the third reason I emphasize home ownership: Your house is the only investment you can really enjoy. People sometimes think of art, jewelry, or collectibles as "investments you can enjoy," but they are not truly marketable investments, because they are sold through dealers and there is too large a spread between the "bid" price and the "asked" price. If you buy a diamond, for example, for $5,000 and then sell it back the next day, you will probably only get 50 cents on the dollar. Homes are recognized as marketable investments, even though relatively illiquid. You can't really cuddle up with your bank passbook or sleep with your stock certificates (OK, you can . . . but please go back and reread the section on financial dysfunction). You can derive tangible enjoyment from your home. I recommend purchasing a home worth 2 to 2.5 times your annual income. If you are

> **Your house is the only investment you can really enjoy . . . . You can't cuddle up with your bank passbook or sleep with your stock certificates.**

earning $40,000 a year, buy a home worth $80,000 to $100,000. Live in that home until its value is equal to 100% to 125% of your annual income. If after 5 years, you are making $75,000 a year and your home is worth $115,000, consider selling it and buying a home worth $150,000 to $180,000. Think of it as trading up. (Note that in most of California, as well as Manhattan, these ratios are about 50% higher.) For most people, the formulas in Exercise 7.3, "What's the Right Value House for You?," apply when it comes to buying a home.

What's the Right Value House for You?

FOR MOST PEOPLE

Your annual income $_____ ×2.5 = $_____

Your annual income $_____ ×2 = $_____

This is the price range your house should be in (total value, not just the mortgage)

FOR PEOPLE LIVING IN MUCH OF THE NORTHEAST OR IN MOST PARTS OF CALIFORNIA

Your annual income $_____ ×3.75 = $_____

Your annual income $_____ ×3 = $_____

This is the price range your house should be in (total value, not just the mortgage)

When Is the Time to Trade Up?

FOR MOST PEOPLE

Your annual income $_____ ×1.5 = $_____

Your annual income $_____ ×1 = $_____

If the fair market value of your house is in or below this range, it's time to think about trading up.

FOR PEOPLE LIVING IN MUCH OF THE NORTHEAST OR IN MOST PARTS OF CALIFORNIA

Your annual income $_____ ×2 = $_____

Your annual income $_____ ×1.25 = $_____

If the fair market value of your house is in or below this range, it's time to think about trading up.

EXERCISE 7.3

Each time you trade up, you generally get a nicer house and a better neighborhood and school district—more tangible enjoyment. Trading up does not have to mean a larger house; it simply means a house valued proportionately to your income. Trading up could mean a smaller house on a lake. As long as the ratio is within the correct range, many options are available.

> Debt can be either a positive or a negative force in building financial peace of mind.

People often ask how much of a down payment they should make. Generally, the ideal amount to put down is 20% of the value. Less than a 20% down payment usually results in the lender requiring you to purchase private mortgage insurance. This means that you must pay an insurance company to issue a policy guaranteeing that the company will make the mortgage payments if you fail to do so, so the lender does not get stuck with the house if you default on the loan. This insurance premium is added to your monthly mortgage payment.

Do whatever is necessary to pull together a 20% down payment. Perhaps you can borrow it from relatives. Your parents may be willing to lend you the money or enter into an equity-sharing agreement with you. Some churches and religious organizations have funds available to help members buy a home. Buying a home is so important that I encourage clients to buy a home even if they don't have a 20% down payment. Your state may offer various types of assistance. FHA and VA loans may be available with little or no down payment required. Often builders offer brand new "starter" homes for as little as 5% down. You also may be able to borrow against your 401(k) or withdraw up to $10,000 from your IRAs with no penalty for the purpose of buying a home.

Buying your first house is so critical to your financial future that you need to just do it! The larger the down payment you have, the larger the selection of houses you will have to choose from. However, if you only have 5% or even 3% to put down, go out and find a house you can buy with that amount down.

The only reason to rent instead of buy is if you know you will not be living in the house for at least 5 years and you aren't interested in renting it out when you move. The transaction costs (realtor commissions, closing costs, etc.) are not likely to be covered by the appreciation in less than 5 years.

Pay Off Credit Card and Consumer Debt

Consumer debt is one of the biggest obstacles to achieving financial health and peace of mind. There are so many dysfunctional beliefs about debt that we financial advisors sometimes throw up our hands in despair. Here's the simple truth: Debt can be either a positive or a negative force in building financial peace of mind. It is often in the foundation stage of life that people either use debt wisely and plan well for the future or use it unwisely and become dysfunctional financial cripples.

Some of us received the message as children that any debt at all was evil. Maybe incurring short-term debt was a necessary evil sometimes, but it was not what "nice people" did. Other families were always in debt, and children in those families grew up believing that calls from bill collectors were a normal part of life. Few of us were taught about "good" debt and "bad" debt.

To be "good" debt, two elements need to be satisfied:

- Whatever is being financed should last longer than the loan.
- Financing should provide positive leverage, which means it enables you to earn more in the future. For example, education loans enable you to get a better job at higher pay; buying a car for basic transportation (in other words, not a Porsche!) enables you to get to work.

If we apply these two criteria to the everyday decisions in your financial life, you can easily see the difference. Complete Exercise 7.4, "Your Attitude toward Debt," to test your own attitudes about debt and then read the following text, keyed to the questions.

Your Attitude Toward Debt

To help you improve your own understanding to debt's double-edged sword, circle your answer, true or false, to the following questions.

Question 1.
You should always pay off your house as fast as possible to save interest expense.

True **or** False

Question 2.
The most important consideration when financing a car is to make sure you can make the payments.

True **or** False

Question 3.
Smart people never borrow money for college expenses.

True **or** False

Question 4.
It's OK to pay for a vacation with a credit card as long as you pay it off in a year.

True **or** False

Question 5.
Financially savvy people have no debt and never lend money.

True **or** False

Question 6.
If you have to borrow money for a car, an 8% car loan is better than using an 8% home equity loan so you don't have a lien on your house.

True **or** False

If you answered "true" to any of these questions, this section may help you sort out the difference between "good" debt and "bad" debt. See the explanation for the correct answers in Question 1 through Question 6 in the text, based on the differences between good debt and bad debt.

EXERCISE 7.4

Why You Should Not Pay Off Your Home
(Answer to Question 1, Exercise 7.4)

Because a house lasts longer than its mortgage, paying off your house as quickly as possible may not be the best use of your money, particularly if you are not taking advantage of all year pension funding opportunities. If you are in a 25% tax bracket, a 6% mortgage actually costs you less than 4.5% after taxes. Over the past 70 years, the stock market has increased an average of 11% per year. Investing $100 a month at that historical rate would net almost $40,000 after capital gains taxes in 15 years. Paying the extra $100 toward a mortgage would save less than $30,000 over the same period.

Thus by investing the money, after 15 years you could pay down the mortgage to where it would have been if you applied $100 a month to the principal. Plus the investment would give you over $10,000 more! Add to this advantage the $4,200+ you would have saved on the additional interest you were able to deduct over the 15 years. This positive leverage suggests that this is good debt and promotes long-term financial freedom.

For many of my clients, paying off their mortgage is a major goal. They maintain that it will give them a sense of security and peace of mind. This belief fits the classic definition of financial dysfunction: financial strategies that people think are effective but actually impede their financial progress.

As Figure 7.3 visually illustrates, it is actually much riskier from an asset allocation standpoint to have a home paid off and few other assets (A) than to have a mortgage and a more balanced investment portfolio (B). The former scenario results in your having too many eggs in one basket, and this lack of diversification can be devastating if real estate values drop. In addition, the lack of liquidity can be traumatic. Keep in mind that if you encounter adverse circumstances (for example, you lose your job or become disabled), the bank is not likely to be willing to loan money on your house. The cartoon in Figure 7.4 is an extreme example of a millionaire who owns his home and the acres of land it sits on—yet must live in poverty because he has no money.

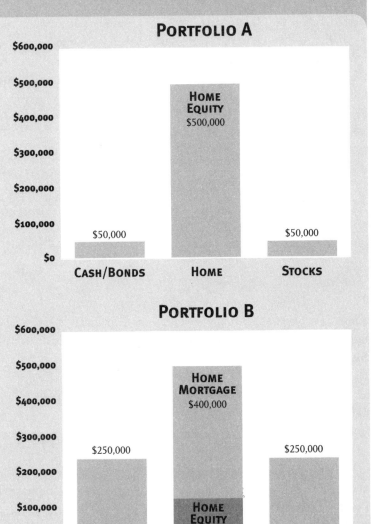

Comparison of Two Portfolios: Which Is Riskier?

PORTFOLIO A

- Cash/Bonds: $50,000
- Home — Home Equity: $500,000
- Stocks: $50,000

PORTFOLIO B

- Cash/Bonds: $250,000
- Home — Home Mortgage: $400,000; Home Equity: $100,000
- Stocks: $250,000

FIGURE 7.3

FIGURE 7.4   "My 80 acres are worth a million bucks!
And by golly, it's free and clear."

We are great believers in the value of the home mortgage for the advantages it provides. In addition to the positive leverage just explained, mortgages offer middle-income Americans an additional buffer against inflation, as well as more financial flexibility. With a fixed-rate mortgage you are protected against future inflation. If inflation increases, your rate remains fixed and you repay the mortgage with cheaper dollars. If interest rates drop, you can refinance. In the worst-case scenario, interest rates stay the same. And you can always pay off your mortgage any time you want.

Why the Life of Your Vehicle Is More Important than the Payment
(Answer to Question 2, Exercise 7.4)
Let's apply these criteria to car loans. If you finance your car for 2 or 3 years, that meets one test for a good loan because your car will probably last longer than the term of the loan. However, if you finance your car for 10 years, it is bad debt, since the debt outlives the purchase.

If you are buying a car to use to get to work, you are gaining positive leverage because you will have more job opportunities and increase your earning potential. It would be bad debt, though, to finance a Porsche instead of a Taurus—because, unless you are in the business of selling Porsches, you don't get any additional leverage from a Porsche (even if you can make the payments).

Why You Should Borrow Money for College
(Answer to Question 3, Exercise 7.4)

What about borrowing money for college? Your education will presumably benefit you over the course of your entire lifetime, so your purchase outlasts your debt. And you are getting positive leverage because the increase in your earning capacity far outstrips the cost of the loan. As we mentioned earlier, it is more important to save when you are young because the government will lend you money for education but not for retirement.

Why You Should Not Buy Short-Lived Purchases on Payment Plans
(Answer to Question 4, Exercise 7.4)

What about borrowing money for furniture or putting your vacation on your credit card? Simply apply the two tests to see if these are good debt or bad debt, remembering that good debt must meet both criteria. Because consumables (such as dinners, clothes, or travel) are used up or depreciate immediately, using any kind of revolving debt to finance these types of consumer goods is bad debt. The credit card balance lingers on after the new sofa is lumpy and tattered and the vacation is nothing but memories. It soon becomes easy to separate the good, the bad, and the ugly.

How Much Debt Is Too Much Debt?
(Answer to Question 5, Exercise 7.4)

Excess debt creates a downward spiral that makes escape increasingly difficult. You can calculate where you are in the spiral by figuring how much consumer debt (i.e., bad debt) you owe as a percentage of your income. To see how much consumer debt you are carrying, fill

Your Consumer Debt List

How much consumer debt are you carrying? Below list every debt used to buy consumables or borrowed for an asset that won't last as long as the debt. Include loans without collateral and debt consolidation loans. Do not include home mortgage or education loans.

Credit Card or Lender Name	Current Balance
1 _____	$ _____
2 _____	$ _____
3 _____	$ _____
4 _____	$ _____
5 _____	$ _____
6 _____	$ _____
7 _____	$ _____
8 _____	$ _____
9 _____	$ _____
10 _____	$ _____
Total debt:	$ _____
Total annual income:	$ _____
Total debt as percentage of income:	_____ %

EXERCISE 7.5

out Exercise 7.5, "Your Consumer Debt." For example, assume that your income is $100,000 a year, and your consumer debt (i.e., bad debt) adds up to $20,000 (20% of income). You are at the point where your debt is a financial problem. To start with, you should stop using credit cards, as noted in Table 7.6.

I wonder how many of you can appreciate the extent that financial dysfunction has overtaken American society. I can assure you that professional financial advisors are dealing with an ever-worsening situation, particularly regarding consumer debt. According to the National Foundation for Credit Counseling, the average American carries roughly $10,000 in credit card debt. Back

Evaluating Your Consumer Debt

Consumer Debt as % of Income*	Amount of Debt, Based on $100,000 Income	Prognosis	Prescription
No consumer debt	$0	Ideal	•No action required
Up to 10%	Less than $10,000	Acceptable	•No action required
10%–25%	$10,000–$25,000	Problem	•Get rid of credit cards •Make a budget •Consolidate your debt
25%–45%	$25,000–$40,000	Trouble	•Make drastic changes •Sell house and downsize •Change to public schools •Take a second job •Begin credit counseling
Over 45%	More than $45,000	Hopeless	•Bankruptcy planning

*Does not include home mortgage or education loans.

TABLE 7.6

in 1990, that figure was about $3,000. Now 83% of college students have credit cards, with an average of 3 cards per student. Their average credit card debt is roughly $2,500. One in 4 students owes more than $3,000. Nearly 10% of students owe more than $7,000, not including student loans.

Should I Get a Car Loan or Use a Home Equity Loan to Buy a Car?
(Answer to Question 6, Exercise 7.4)

If the interest rate on a car loan and the rate on your home equity line of credit are the same, you are better off using your home equity loan. That's because the interest on up to $100,000 borrowed on your home over its cost is normally tax deductible, whereas the interest paid on a car loan is not deductible (unless you use it more than 50% of the time for business). Sometimes auto companies offer very low rates, or even zero interest, during special promotions. In those cases it may be advantageous to forego the tax-deductible loan and take the lower rate car loan. However, be aware that often in those promotions they offer a so-called "cash rebate" if you pay cash instead of taking the low-rate car loan. The "cash rebate" is actually prepaid interest, because if you opt for the loan you give up the cash rebate.

If you divide the cash rebate by the number of months for which you are financing the car, you will know how much interest on average you are actually paying in prepaid interest if you use the auto manufacturer's car loan. Multiplying the monthly prepaid interest by 12 gives you the annual prepaid interest, and then dividing that by half of the amount you are borrowing will give you a close estimate of the real annual interest rate that the prepaid interest represents.

For example, what should you do if you have a choice of either (1) buying a $24,000 car for zero down and zero interest over 24 months or (2) paying cash and getting a $2,400 "cash rebate" so that all you have to pay is $21,600? The $2,400 rebate over 24 months means that the prepaid interest is $100 a month, or $1,200 a year. Half the amount of the loan is $12,000. Dividing the annual prepaid interest of $1,200 by half of the amount of the loan ($12,000) shows that you are actually paying 10% interest per year. Certainly, in that case you would be better off borrowing $21,600 from your 8% home equity loan so you can buy the car for cash, rather than financing with a car loan with what is mistakenly described as "zero interest."

The five fundamentals of financial fitness just discussed are the key financial strategies you need to build a firm financial foundation. If you ignore any of these five fundamentals, your financial progress will be impeded later in life. Once the foundation is laid, we proceed to the early accumulation stage.

Early Accumulation

At the point when your net worth exceeds your annual income—usually between ages 30 and 40—you move into the early accumulation stage of the Financial Life Cycle. This is where basic investment begins. At this point we teach clients how to diversify their assets.

There are three categories of assets: stocks, bonds, and real estate. Most people know that real estate consists of land and any buildings on the land. Many people, however, aren't clear about the difference between stocks and bonds, so I'll explain that here simply and briefly.

Think of it this way: If I am starting a business and need capital (money to start the business), I might come to you and ask to borrow $10,000 for 5 years at 10% interest. If you agree, your investment would be a bond. I am legally required to pay you $1,000 a year as interest for 5 years, and then to repay the initial $10,000 in full. If I am unable to repay this debt, I must declare bankruptcy. That's how bonds work.

If, on the other hand, I offer to sell you 10% of my company for $10,000, and you agree, then I have sold you stock in my company. I am not legally required to pay you back—ever—and I don't have to pay you any interest on the $10,000 you invested. However, if my company makes a profit, you are entitled to 10% of those profits, which are paid out as dividends. Moreover, you can sell the stock to anyone else. You may not get any money back, or that $10,000 investment could end up being worth a million dollars at some point if my name were Bill Gates.

When you make an investment in something that is interest earning, like a bond, you are a *loaner* When you make an investment in equities, or stock, you are an *owner*. *Interest-earning assets* include bonds and cash; *equities* refer to stocks and mutual funds that hold stock.

The major lesson I have learned during my career as a financial advisor is that the mandate to diversify investments to include stocks, bonds, and real estate is inviolate. I don't care how people feel about their Ford stock because they've worked there forever. I don't care about tax consequences. I don't care how high a client thinks the stock will go. I don't care how much money the stock has lost. The consequences of failing to diversify are so tremendous in our fast-moving economy that I preach diversification as a universal imperative. I've seen too many undiversified portfolios wiped out in the blink of an eye.

> **The major lesson I have learned during my career as a financial advisor is that the mandate to diversify investments to include stocks, bonds, and real estate is inviolate.**

Let me give you an example of a well-meaning client who never diversified. In the late 1970s, I worked with Suzanne, a semiretired client who had lived through the Depression. She had seen her parents lose the family fortune in the stock market crash of 1929. Suzanne absolutely refused to put any of her money in the stock market, and she insisted on keeping all her money in bonds and CDs. She would spend her time going from bank to bank every quarter trying to get the best CD rate offered, and she filled her portfolio with maturity bonds and corporate bonds with the highest yields.

Suzanne also used brokers who talked her into buying bond mutual funds (as you might expect, these are mutual funds that invest in bonds). As the runaway inflation of the 1970s peaked at 15%, she saw the values of her bond funds plummet. The 3% or 4% rate she had locked in on her individual bonds was completely inadequate to keep pace with inflation. Yet the liquidation of the bonds or bond funds would mean a devastating loss to her accumulated capital.

In 1978 she took the loss and decided that the safe place to be was in money market funds, which at that time were paying about 9%, and where there was virtually no possibility of losing her principal. She felt that at 9% she would have adequate cash flow and still protect her principal.

Ten years later, when she came to see us, money market funds were paying only 3%. Her income had been cut by more than 60%.

Although inflation had subsided from 15% to 2%, her cost of living had not dropped in proportion to either inflation or her income.

You will recognize Suzanne as fitting the miser personality (a saver motivated by fear) as discussed in Chapter 4. What she needed was some basic financial education. I taught her the risk/reward relationship and the basics of modern portfolio theory (see Chapter 5). Then it was easy for her to see that if she had had more balanced investments (with part in cash, part in bonds, and part in stocks) over the long term, her portfolio would have been substantially less risky. At the same time it would be generating a much higher return than she could receive by relying only on one asset class to carry her through to her financial goals.

Diversification starts with real estate, which is why we stress buying the right-size house in building the foundation stage of life. Once the real estate piece is in place, you can begin creating an investment portfolio and start diversifying between interest-earning assets and equity assets.

A lot of basic investment education occurs during this early accumulation stage. Not understanding the basics doesn't mean that you are hopelessly dysfunctional; it only means that you need a financial coach. For example, as I said earlier, I need reeducation about interpreting my blood pressure results every year. Likewise, my clients need ongoing education about asset classes and their function. (For the principles of Functional Asset Allocation, see Chapter 8.)

Rapid Accumulation

Usually between ages 40 and 50, when our net worth reaches 3 times our annual income, our investment income exceeds our annual savings. Then we move into the rapid accumulation stage, where our net worth tends to increase exponentially and our estate is truly created. At this stage it is most appropriate to increase the level of risk and concentrate on the tax efficiency of our portfolio.

A key strategy to increase tax efficiency is optimizing the use of investment vehicles available. The main issue we must address to make a portfolio tax-efficient is "asset location," which refers to how after-tax (i.e., nonqualified) money should be invested versus qualified money (i.e., pension accounts) versus investments in Roth-type accounts. (We'll explore each of these in detail shortly.) Other issues include identifying where money managers can add value and the tax efficiency of individual investments.

Remember that each stage of the Financial Life Cycle is built on the preceding stage. We do not want to achieve tax efficiency at the expense of diversification, and both tax efficiency and diversification take a back seat to the five fundamentals of fiscal fitness. If a client fit into this rapid accumulation stage based on income and net worth but had not yet purchased a home, I would recommend buying a home next, even if it meant a less diversified portfolio. Then we would again be able to address diversification and tax efficiency.

Let's assume that you have met the five fundamentals and diversified your portfolio appropriately. If you want to achieve financial fitness and freedom, your next step is to begin looking at what type of investment to hold in which investment vehicle.

Nonqualified assets are those purchased with after-tax money. An example would be using a bonus from your employer (which is added to your W-2 wages) to buy a CD or shares in a mutual fund. The money is taxed before it is invested. Interest paid on nonqualified assets, such as bonds, CDs, or savings accounts, is generally taxed at regular income tax rates—so if you are in the 15% bracket, you pay 15%; if you're in the 28% bracket, then you pay 28%, and so on. Earnings from dividends (of U.S. corporations) and gains you make on the sale of nonqualified assets, like real estate or mutual funds, are generally taxed as capital gains. The capital gains tax rate imposed depends both on your tax bracket and on the length of time you have held the investment or asset. Long-term capital gains rates for investments held more than a year are 30% to 50% lower than ordinary income rates. So it is a terrific advantage to have investment income taxed as long-term capital gains.

Although nonqualified assets are afforded no special tax provisions as a class in general, specific individual investments do offer tax deferral or shelter. For instance, U.S. savings bonds give you the option of declaring the interest annually as accrued or deferring the declaration of interest until you redeem the bonds. When redeemed, the interest is nontaxable to the state and may even be nontaxable federally, depending on how you use the proceeds. For example, if you buy U.S. Savings Bonds in your name, or as a co-owner with your spouse, you can cash them in when your children go to college. The accrued interest then may be tax-exempt, depending on your income.

Municipal bonds pay interest that can be fully exempt from federal and state income tax. Stock options give you the right to buy a certain number of shares of a stock at a fixed price (the "strike price") before a certain date. Paper profits from stock options generally are taxed when the option is exercised, i.e., when you buy the stock at the "strike price" before the options expire. However, incentive stock options (ISOs), stock options in your company issued as part of your compensation package to improve company performance, are not taxable when exercised, but may be subject to alternate minimum tax. These considerations may require professional advice.

Qualified assets, such as 401(k) and pension plans, are purchased with pretax dollars and grow on a tax-deferred basis. You don't have to pay income tax on the earnings or profits generated within a pension account until you make withdrawals from the pension. When you withdraw money from a pension account, it is taxed at regular income tax rates.

Roth-type assets are those purchased with after-tax dollars, but then they grow on a tax-free basis. These include Roth IRAs as well as several quasi-Roth vehicles such as Education IRAs and Section 529 plans. These quasi-Roth vehicles are savings plans specifically geared to use to save for a child's college education. The contributions to these savings plans are not deductible, but the earnings accrued on investments in the plans are free from taxes if the money is ultimately used for higher education. This tax-free compounding becomes meaningful when you have an investment horizon of at least 10 years.

Table 7.7 summarizes these different types of assets.

So what does all this add up to in terms of tax efficiency? The obvious benefit of putting money into a pension plan is that the investment grows on a tax-deferred basis. The advantage of investing in

Investment Vehicles and Optimum Asset Location

Type	Examples	Characteristics	Ideal Investments
Qualified assets	•Deductible IRA •401(k) •403(b) •SEP •SIMPLE	•Bought with pretax dollars •Grow tax-deferred •Can't take income as capital gains	Interest-earning investments, such as bonds, bond mutual funds, CDs
Nonqualified assets	•Joint accounts •Non-IRA brokerage accounts •"Transfer on Death" accounts	•Bought with after-tax dollars (costs more to invest) •Interest, dividends taxed yearly •Can take growth as capital gain, paying less tax	Stocks and stock mutual funds, especially large cap
Roth & quasi-Roth assets	•Roth IRAs •529 plans* •Coverdell ESAs*	•Bought with after-tax dollars •Grow tax-free, not just tax-deferred •Good if time horizon exceeds 10 years	Small cap and foreign stocks and stock mutual funds

*If used for college education.

TABLE 7.7

capital assets (mutual funds and stocks) is that you don't have to pay taxes on the appreciation until you choose to sell them. Thus they also grow on a tax-deferred basis.

To the extent that you put capital assets into a pension account, the tax advantages of investing in capital assets and using a pension plan become redundant. Everything you withdraw from a pension account, including dividends and capital gains on stock, is taxable at your regular rate—up to 35%. If you buy the stocks for your portfolio outside your pension, however, the dividends and long-term capital gains are taxed at the capital gains rate, which is no more than 15%.

So should you invest your pension funds in equities (i.e., stocks and mutual funds) or in interest-earning investments (i.e., cash and bonds)? Consider the investment portfolio shown in Table 7.8, "Asset Location Matters."

Qualified Assets: pension funds (401k, IRAs)	$100,000
Nonqualified Assets: (after-tax) money	$100,000
Total investments	$200,000

Table 7.8 shows two possible ways to invest the money for the next 30 years. Plan A suggests investing the pension money in stocks and investing the after-tax funds in bonds. Plan B suggests investing the pension money in treasury bills and investing the after-tax money in stocks. The result is that after 30 years (taking into account the tax implications) the tax-efficient portfolio (Plan B) produces a 15% higher after-tax rate of return! The return assumptions are listed in the table; the tax assumptions are a combination of federal and state taxes on income and capital gains. In this example, the current income tax rates are 35% federal and 5% state (40% combined). After 30 years, they decrease to 25% and 5%, respectively (30% combined). The capital gains tax remains constant at 15% federal and 5% state (20% combined).

Most advisors would not recommend buying tax-exempt municipal bonds in an IRA. Here's why: The interest generated by a municipal bond is exempt from federal income taxes and state income taxes (in the state issuing the bond). When you buy a municipal bond in an IRA, you are converting tax-free income into income that will eventually be taxed. To a lesser extent, but on the same principle, when you are putting capital assets into a pension plan you are converting what could be taxed as capital gains into ordinary income, which is taxable at a higher rate.

As you begin to understand the significance of this concept, it becomes readily apparent that a blatant malpractice in the financial services industry has been the sale of annuities in pension accounts. Annuities may have an appropriate place in a very limited number of situations, but they tend to be very heavily marketed because they pay generous

> **Annuities tend to be very heavily marketed because they pay generous commissions to the annuities salesperson.**

commissions to the annuities salesperson. The advantage of the annuity is that the earnings accrue on a tax-deferred basis. To hold pension money in an annuity is 100% redundant because money in a pension account is already sheltered. When you factor in the high costs of an annuity, the difference in long-term performance as opposed to purchasing mutual funds (even in the same fund family) is phenomenal.

Roth-type accounts are one of the few bright spots on the financial horizon—where Congress has seen fit to improve the financial fitness of Americans while it loads us under with more tax bills and complexity. The great feature of a Roth account is that the money invested can come out tax free anytime. During retirement there are no minimum distributions, and accrued earnings can be withdrawn totally tax free. You get the benefits of tax-free accumulation forever and can pass it on to your spouse or children with no income tax consequences whatsoever.

Yet even these investment accounts have the potential to disrupt your financial freedom. Because all your earnings and gains will be tax free, you want to gain as much profit as possible from your Roth. However, because you have already paid tax on the money and will not be allowed to write off any losses, you really do not want to lose money on your Roth investments. This is why we recommend very long-term investments for Roth money. Small cap and international investments are particularly well suited for Roth and quasi-Roth accounts. "Quasi-Roth" investment vehicles are those which, like Roths,

Asset Location Matters:
Usual Portfolio Construction Versus a
Tax-Efficient Portfolio

Nonqualified Assets: After-Tax Money	$100,000
Qualified Assets: Pension Funds (401k, IRAs)	$100,000
Total:	$200,000

Plan A

INVEST THE AFTER-TAX MONEY IN MUNICIPAL BONDS AND THE PENSION FUNDS IN STOCKS.

		Original Investment	30 Years Later
Nonqualified (after tax)	**INTEREST EARNING**		
	Municipals	$100,000	
	30-year return	3.35%	$272,808
	Taxes	0%	$0
	Total after taxes		$272,808
Qualified (pension funds)	**EQUITY INVESTMENTS**		
	Stocks	$100,000	
	30-year return	9.60%	$1,761,131
	Taxes	30%	$538,339
	Total after taxes		$1,232,792
	Combined total		$1,505,600

TABLE 7.8

are funded with after-tax money and provide tax-deferred accumulation of earnings, but tax-free withdrawals are more restricted—for example, they might have to be used for college.

Asset Location Matters, *continued*

Nonqualified Assets: After-Tax Money	$100,000
Qualified Assets: Pension Funds (401k, IRAs)	$100,000
Total:	$200,000

Plan B

INVEST THE AFTER-TAX MONEY IN STOCKS AND THE PENSION FUNDS IN TREASURIES.

		Original Investment	30 Years Later
Nonqualified (after tax)	**EQUITY INVESTMENTS**		
	Stocks	$100,000	
	30-year return	9.60%	$1,761,131
	Taxes	20%	$352,226
	Total after taxes		$1,408,905
Qualified (pension funds)	**INTEREST EARNING**		
	Treasuries	$100,000	
	30-year return	5.00%	$446,774
	Taxes	30%	$134,032
	Total after taxes		$312,742
		Combined total	$1,721,647

PLAN B BEATS PLAN A BY $216,047 OR 14%

THE CONSERVATION YEARS

From all that has been written about retirement planning, you would think that most people are eager to leave work and retire to play golf for the rest of their days. In my practice, I have found that most clients are not interested in retiring as such, but they are very motivated to achieve financial independence.

Retiring has a connotation of being put out to pasture. Indeed, when many people retire, they feel useless and irrelevant. In our society many people have built their self-esteem around their business card. So we emphasize financial independence as a transitional goal—

The Conservation Stages of the Financial Life Cycle

Stage	Financial Independence	Conservation
Age	50–70	70–85
Financial Criteria	Investment earnings equal 50% or more of living costs	Live off investment earnings plus retirement pension
Investment Portfolio	7–10 times annual living expense	10–15 times annual living expense
Strategy	Transitional stage: start doing what you really like to do, start business, semiretire, etc. Supplement earnings with investment income	Capital preservation, lower-risk
Asset Allocation	50% interest-earning/ 50% equities	60% interest-earning/ 40% equities

TABLE 7.9

working at your own pace, either in a business you start yourself, part time in your current employment, or perhaps as a consultant (see Table 7.9).

During the financial independence stage, you continue to earn money, but you supplement your earned income with money from your investments to maintain your standard of living. When you decide to stop working completely, and rely totally on your investment income, you enter the conservation stage.

Financial Independence

The first criterion for entering this stage is to have established a standard of living you are comfortable with for the rest of your life. The biggest long-term risk for most people is not the risk of their cost of living increasing (through inflation, for example) as time goes on, but constantly expecting to increase their standard of living.

In other words, you can't afford to enter the financial independence stage until you have put your children through college, you have bought as expensive a house as you will ever want, and you are prepared to settle in the future for the same standard of living you have already achieved.

> Generally, I find that monthly living costs run about 4 times a person's monthly house payment.

For this reason we change to a long-term view to evaluate the sufficiency of our clients' portfolios. We define the necessary investment portfolio as a multiple of living expenses, instead of net worth as a multiple of income, as we did in the earlier stages.

The ideal investment portfolio at this stage includes stocks, bonds, and cash. Here we normally look at an individual having an investment portfolio of 7 to 10 times her annual living expenses. The exact multiple would depend on how much money she earns because the income from her investments is designed to be supplemental.

One of the biggest satisfactions in my job as a financial advisor is helping people who come to me ready to make a change. They are tired of working at what they are doing and want more options. For example, a few years ago, Lisa was burned out from working in a large education bureaucracy, but she had saved nowhere near enough money to retire completely. She was only 53 years old, 12 years away from receiving any kind of meaningful pension or Social Security income.

When I asked Lisa the key question of how much it cost her to live, she was at a complete loss. I find it interesting that when asked that question, people seldom know the answer. They almost always know how much they earn; less often they know their net worth or the value of their investment portfolio. Sometimes they know how much they pay in taxes, and they usually can quickly figure out how they are saving. But almost inevitably they are stumped when asked how much it costs to maintain their current standard of living.

> **Once they start doing what they really love, people may end up making more money working part time than they did before working full time!**

Over the years, I have developed a few rules of thumb about the cost of living. Generally, I find that monthly living costs run about 4 times a person's monthly house payment. Your standard of living tends to be directly related to the value of your house. People who live in more expensive houses invariably have a total higher standard of living than people who live in less expensive houses. I believe this is because many of our expectations are socially contextual. Although we may not consciously keep up with the Joneses, the makes of the cars the people in our neighborhood drive and the schools they send their children to send subtle messages. The type of furniture they have and the kinds of vacations they take invariably influence us to a much greater degree than we realize.

For Lisa, the educator, the starting point was to look at how much it cost her to live. Although she was earning $80,000 a year, Lisa's actual cost of living was $4,500 a month, or approximately $54,000 a year. The rest of her income went to taxes and savings.

In order to produce the kind of cash flow she needed to retire completely, she would need to have an investment portfolio of a million dollars (i.e., 10 to 15 times her annual living expenses, as explained in the next section on the conservation stage). Because Lisa had only $250,000 in investments, she felt it was hopeless.

Her situation gave me an opportunity to apply a financial fix that solved what seemed to be an unsolvable problem. I was able to show her that by downsizing from the $200,000 condo she lived in and moving to a small town in Florida near her parents, she could buy a very nice smaller condo on the beach for $80,000. With 20% down ($16,000), her monthly payments would be around $600, including principal, interest, taxes, and insurance. With that lifestyle, she would need only about $2,500 a month to live, or $30,000 a year. Her investments, at a 7% rate of return, would generate $17,000 to $18,000 of that total. She could easily earn $12,000 to $15,000 a year as a part-time teacher, which was her true love. Lisa is able to live the kind of life she wanted by a relatively simple process of downsizing.

Over the years, I have often found that when people decide to become financially independent and accept the notion of downsizing, they may need to accompany the change with a move to a different geographical area. Selecting the right-size house is the key consideration for them.

Let's look at another situation that financial advisors frequently see. Paul came to me about 10 years ago looking for a financial advisor. He was fed up with his job at a nonprofit organization. It would cost him about $90,000 a year to maintain his standard of living. He had $900,000 in investment assets. At age 63, he would still have to earn about $5,000 a month to continue saving 10% of his income, pay his taxes, and have $90,000 a year to live on. It was a revelation to him when Paul realized that he could easily make $60,000 a year working part time as a consultant at $100 to $150 an hour. However, I warned him about the unanticipated consequence often experienced by those taking the plunge into financial independence. Once they start doing what they really love, they may end up making more money working part time than they did before working full time!

What actually happens? I believe that when people unleash the entrepreneurial spirit within them and can spend their time doing what they are truly good at, they come to fully realize their unique abilities. They are able to create much more value in the world, and their consulting clients pay for that added value. They enjoy life more while working fewer hours and earning more money.

From a portfolio standpoint, our objectives during the financial independence stage are to rebalance the portfolio aggressively and build a bond ladder—a strategy of buying bonds in an annual series so that one comes due each year (for details, see Chapter 8). The bond ladder gives clients the necessary cash flow to supplement their pension or Social Security income in order to maintain their lifestyle for 15 years. All other things being equal, in the financial independence stage we normally recommend that people maintain, in their investment portfolio, a balance of 50% interest-earning investments (bonds and cash) and 50% equities (stocks and mutual funds).

In earlier stages, such as the building the foundation and the early accumulation stages, rebalancing is necessary only once a year. (Rebalancing is a check to determine if your portfolio is adequately diversified among the asset categories of stocks, bonds, and real estate.) As assets grow in the rapid accumulation stage, we look to rebalance the portfolio twice a year. With many of our long-time clients who are in the financial independence stage of life, especially when assets exceed a million dollars, we recommend rebalancing quarterly.

Conservation

The conservation stage begins when you decide to stop working altogether, which occurs most commonly between the ages of 60 and 70. At this point, a household's investment portfolio should add up to 10 to 15 times your annual living expenses (depending on how much pension and Social Security income you can count on). Conventional wisdom maintains that retired people need only 80% of their preretirement income. When I help clients plan for retirement, however, they generally want to maintain their current lifestyle. I help them accomplish this goal by using earnings from their investments to supplement pension and Social Security income. This stage calls for a more conservative investment mix, and normally our default position drops from the 50/50 balance of the financial independence stage to one of 60% interest earning and 40% equities. The key strategy we focus on here is capital preservation, or making sure the portfolio is maintained with minimal volatility so that we don't risk losing the nest egg.

Some people have difficulty understanding the significance of what they have achieved financially. A prospective new client in this conservation phase came to see me after interviewing several other financial advisors. His first question to me was "What kind of rate of return can you get for me?"

> **Some people have difficulty understanding the significance of what they have achieved financially.**

I looked at his situation and noted that it was costing him about $50,000 a year to live. He had a portfolio of about a million dollars that, at a conservative 7% rate of return, would generate $70,000 of income annually. He was receiving about $25,000 a year from Social Security and another $10,000 a year from a pension. With a total income of $105,000, and allowing $30,000 a year for taxes and permanent savings, he still had a surplus of $25,000 a year over and above what he was currently spending!

I explained to him that he was using the wrong question to evaluate a financial advisor. He already had more money than he would ever spend. Sure, I could show him how to get a 15% to 25% return on his investments, but even if he did that and doubled his money within the next 3 to 5 years, it wouldn't change the way he was living. But if he took that much of a risk, and ended up losing half his money, he would be forced to live very differently. There was no longer any upside to his taking risks. What he really needed from me or some other responsible financial advisor was the permission to spend the money he already had. His wife's eyes lit up, and he looked at her and smiled. I explained how I would figure out how much they could spend without ever running out of money, and implemented an investment strategy to make sure they always had a reliable cash flow.

The most common financial problem I see in the conservation stage is people taking inappropriate risks for their stage in life. Often, this shows up in their having very substantial portfolios yet living at only 25% to 50% of the standard of living at which they can actually afford to live. At the other extreme are those with very undiversified portfolios (e.g., all CDs), who are fearful that they will run out of money so they try to budget themselves to live only on their pension and Social Security (and even saving part of that). The first extreme is a client who needs permission to spend; the other extreme is a client who needs an education in the importance of diversification.

> **The most common financial problem I see in the conservation stage is people taking inappropriate risks for their stage in life.**

This is why we skew the portfolio to provide capital preservation. Frankly, at this point, if people are not able to maintain their standard of living based on their current assets, they must deal with the discrepancy through downsizing and decreasing their cost of living rather than by trying to increase the rate of return from their portfolio. You cannot expect to be able to increase your standard of living meaningfully through better investments—you run the risk of losing a substantial part of your investment portfolio without the investment time horizon left to recover.

The most effective advice I can give retirees is simply to continue to save 10% of their total income, even after retirement. This provides a buffer against inflation, ensures that you will never run out of money, and forces you to live within your means. Moreover, since your portfolio is always growing, you are better able to cope with high nursing home costs or medical costs that may arise near life's end.

I recommend that only select clients consider buying long-term care insurance. First, the client should be at least 60 years old; otherwise, the policy is likely to be out-of-date by the time he needs it, since the government is constantly making changes in this area.

Second, I recommend buying this insurance only when the client has an investment portfolio of between $250,000 and $1 million. If he has less than that, he can't afford long-term care insurance; if he has more than a million dollars, he can insure himself. Many times a person's cost of living decreases in a nursing home because he can't spend money anywhere else.

Most of my clients are shocked to discover that I do *not* consider inflation the bogeyman that many other advisors describe. I believe a well-constructed portfolio that follows the principles of Functional Asset Allocation will protect you against the extremes of both inflation and deflation. Once that is accomplished, I find that most people, especially older people, adapt very well to inflationary pressures.

Here are my 10 reasons why inflation is not a bogeyman:

1. The consumer price index (CPI), which the government calculates to measure inflation, is calculated incorrectly and highly overstated. Even the government now recognizes this.

2. The CPI does not reflect the cost of living, particularly in this stage, because it is heavily driven by housing, education, and medical costs. With retired people owning their homes, finished with their careers, and covered by Medicare, these costs are not relevant to their cost of living.

3. Older people tend to be very good at adjusting their standard of living. When the price of beef goes up, they buy chicken.

4. After retirement, as people age, it usually costs them less to live. They travel less as they become less mobile, and they cut back on shopping for clothes, furniture, etc. They also drive fewer miles, so they can keep their cars longer.

My 10 reasons why inflation is not a bogeyman, *continued*

5. We insist that our clients continue to save 10% throughout their lifetime, which serves as a buffer against inflation.

6. Social Security and many pensions are already overadjusted for inflation.

7. It used to be that interest rates were regulated at a fixed rate. Today, as opposed to the early 1970s, yields on interest-earning investments are themselves very interest-rate sensitive. When inflation increases, the federal reserve increases interest rates. So if you adjust costs for inflation, you must also adjust the yield you are assuming accordingly.

8. A properly balanced portfolio, which includes leveraged real estate, using Functional Asset Allocation (see Chapter 8), generally provides the best protection against inflation.

9. Small changes in inflation rate assumptions produce too wide a span of possibilities over a long period (e.g., 20 to 40 years) to be a useful planning tool.

10. Financial planning should not be approached like an engineering problem. It is a process, not an event. This process takes into account that most changes causing variation in the plan are endogenous (like illness, deaths, divorce, etc.), not exogenous, like inflation. Thus a good financial plan should be dynamic: reviewed every year and updated, with adjustments made for new circumstances. Based on my experience, which includes looking back at assumptions common in the 1970s, designing a financial plan based on static assumptions over the long term inevitably becomes meaningless.

THE LARGESS YEARS

The largess and sunset stages are the final two stages in the Financial Life Cycle.

Largess

If we continue saving, we eventually reach the point where our investment portfolio exceeds 15 times our annual living expenses. We are faced with the reality that we have more money than we could possibly spend in our lifetime and so enter the largess stage (see Table 7.10).

Here are three possible solutions if you have too much money:

1. Spend it down by increasing your standard of living or developing some new bad habits.
2. Gift it away to your children or to charities.
3. Let the government take half of it away from you when you die.

When counseling people in this stage, I first make sure they have everything they want. It is amazing to me how many people have saved and accumulated a substantial estate and still have not done what they have always wanted to do.

Part of this, as previously mentioned, involves giving people permission to spend, but let me mention two other strategies I have found to be effective. The first is to develop a cash cushion and the second is to invest in memories.

A Cash Cushion Cure for Deprivation Anxiety

I have discovered just within the past couple of years that clients with substantial means undergo a very traumatic metamorphosis (which I call *deprivation anxiety*) if they run out of cash. For some reason, running out of cash does not produce as high a level of anxiety in

The Largess Stages of the Financial Life Cycle

Stage	Largess	Sunset
Age	85+	N/A
Financial Criteria	Have more money than can spend in a lifetime	Less than 12 months to live
Investment Portfolio	More than 15 times annual living expense	N/A
Strategy	Start giving money away to kids, charities, etc.	Distribute assets, reduce estate
Asset Allocation	75% interest-earning/ 25% equities	N/A

TABLE 7.10

those individuals in the accumulation stages, but those in the financial independence, conservation, and largess stages are acutely affected. They may be wealthy, they may have substantial assets, but if they do not have enough money in their checking account, it affects their relationships, and causes sleeplessness and other symptoms of extreme anxiety. Couples start bickering over small purchases, criticize each other's spending, and generally put themselves into financial deprivation mode.

One of the primary objectives I set for clients in the largess stage is to develop a cash cushion equal to at least 6 times their monthly living expenses. Having this much cash in a money market account may not be considered smart from an investment standpoint, but from a psychological standpoint it is critical to giving older people, especially those with substantial means, a feeling of comfort.

Note that this is a different standard than I explained earlier in this chapter, where we discussed liquidity and the need for retired people to keep 30% of their annual income in liquid assets. To deal with deprivation anxiety, I increase the base liquidity to 6 times their monthly living expenses. Base liquidity is specifically noted as being immediately accessible. It is not that the funds are technically accessible (such as a short-term bond fund), but these are funds available right now to write a check against.

Deprivation anxiety is especially destructive for those needing permission to spend. There is no way they will spend any money if they are feeling cash-poor.

Investing in Memories

Investing in memories is the second effective strategy for people in the largess stage. This involves planning trips or other events with children and grandchildren, rather than giving outright gifts. People can enjoy the company of their family while at the same time exposing them to new places, concepts, and ideas. Investing in memories is a pleasurable as well as a memorable experience.

The largess stage can be very difficult for some people. They may be very reluctant to let go of their money. Many older people don't understand that, under our current tax system, they (or, more accurately, their estate) will be punished for holding on to it. Of course, the biggest challenge in this stage for those who have achieved wealth is how to pass it on to their children. The hope is that their descendants will use the wealth in a way that will enable them to leverage it and accomplish what they could not otherwise accomplish. The danger is that it may undermine the character of the next generation, and they will squander the opportunities available to them.

> The biggest challenge in this stage for those who have achieved wealth is how to pass it on to their children.

The transfer of wealth from one generation to another is perhaps the most vexing challenge that clients and their financial advisors face.

The strategies employed to accomplish this transfer of wealth—estate planning—are extremely complex, and Congress seems intent on making them more complicated by passing laws every few years incorporating changes that may later be revoked. The complexity today is notoriously used as a sales tool by life insurance agents. They are adept at arranging the numbers (income and estate taxes, investment returns, the value of tax deferral) so the average person is baffled. Somehow it looks as if the financial consumer will come out way ahead on a so-called life insurance investment and still have plenty left over to pay generous commissions and yearly fees. It is very difficult to refute this quackery if you don't understand how the various tax law provisions work in the first place and are not knowledgeable enough to challenge the salespeople's assumptions.

As if that weren't bad enough, we also have to find ways to educate the next generation. The recipients of the wealth must learn to handle it responsibly, so it doesn't magnify any financial problems they may already have. Our own approach has been to recommend that clients in this stage begin a regular gifting program to their children. This can help the next generation gradually accustom themselves to utilizing wealth.

Of course, you can follow this basic program on your own. However, you must accept the reality that your children (or other recipients) are not likely to use the money the same way you would. It is easy to become unhappy, disappointed, and even angry over the ways your children misuse money. But I have seen that it is usually better to gift them $10,000 a year and let them waste it for a few years, getting it all out of their system, rather than dumping a large pile of money on them later when you die. Managing money wisely is learned through experience—like riding a bike. I do not believe anyone can explain to you how to ride a bike. In order to ride the bike, you must ride it yourself. Likewise, no one can explain to you how to use wealth to optimize your own self-actualization. All of us must learn how to do that on our own.

> "You must accept the reality that your children are not likely to use the money the same way you would."

I see many people in their sixties and
seventies with substantial estates who are very
reluctant to make gifts to their children in their
thirties and forties. Usually, when they are in
their eighties and the children in their fifties,
they are still resistant to gifting. Eventually,
perhaps in their nineties, they die and their
children finally receive the benefit of a large
amount of cash. But the children by then are
eligible to receive Social Security, and the inheritance from their parents does them very little good. Had they been
able to utilize this wealth during their foundation years to improve their
lives in their thirties and to send their children to better schools or buy
larger homes, it could have made a very significant difference in their lives.

> In our practice,
> we believe
> simple is
> better when
> it comes to
> estate tax
> planning.

In our practice, we believe simple is better when it comes to estate
tax planning. Estate planning can be complicated to understand and
impossible to implement without the help of a professional.
Unfortunately, the client who opts for a complex arrangement of trusts,
bypasses, and generation-skipping devices usually doesn't have the
slightest idea three days later what those arrangements were.

Estate planning attorneys are seldom geared to follow up with
clients. As a result, trusts are not funded properly or updated as
needed, and they create a false sense of security in clients who think
everything is fine now because they paid a few thousand dollars to set
up a trust. Upon their death, their survivors find out that the estate is
a mess and it can often be more expensive to unwind and pay taxes
than if the client had died with a simple will.

It is easy to strike fear in the hearts of clients by pointing out how
much they would owe in estate taxes if a couple were to die together.
The probability of this happening is grossly exaggerated in most
people's minds. However, it is an effective way to sell life insurance so
money is available to pay the estate tax. Frankly, you have a
statistically greater likelihood of winning the lottery than you do of
being killed together with your spouse, and I certainly don't advise
creating a trust to protect you in case you win the lottery!

In truth, the life insurance for this eventuality only makes sense if much of the estate is illiquid (for example, in real estate or a small business). Unless structured properly and maintained, the insurance proceeds could become part of the estate, thus exacerbating the estate tax problem.

The trust-production industry, of course, has a stake in selling fear and guilt to motivate people to set up trusts. Often, there is a true benefit in creating a trust, but not if the client doesn't understand it. In many states, notably California, a shady industry specializes in so-called trust seminars, which trick people into thinking they need a trust. This gives salespeople an opportunity to find out how much and where attendees' money is, so they can sell the suckers annuities.

There are legitimate uses for trusts. They can provide significant estate tax savings for wealthier families, and in many states (like California) can substantially reduce probate costs. They are especially useful if you want to provide for a handicapped child, or protect part of your estate from your spouse's possible new marriage partner after you die. If your estate is under $2 million (the amount currently exempt from federal estate taxes), however, it is not likely that a trust will be cost effective.

If you do decide to set up a trust, it is imperative to make a lifelong commitment at the same time to have the trust reviewed and revised every other year, knowing that may cost more than $500 each time. Since trusts are very complex, they can quickly go out of date. As a result, too often assets aren't titled correctly, trustee appointments aren't reviewed, and other problems ensue. My distaste for trusts largely stems from seeing too many cases where a client's parents died with stale trusts that were never updated. In that case, probate is more expensive than it would have been with a simple will. Trusts also have to be updated if the law changes, if you modify your life situation (for example, you get divorced), or if you change your mind about how you would like to distribute your assets.

As our clients enter this stage of the Financial Life Cycle, we start by simplifying the investment portfolio. From an investment standpoint, in the largest stage we recommend that investments in the estate be consolidated and heavily oriented toward relatively straightforward interest-earning vehicles. This not only greatly simplifies the estate planning process and ultimate distribution upon death, but it also enables people to avail themselves of a number of options to meet their choice of legacy.

Charitable Gifting Options

One option is a charitable annuity. Charitable annuities enable a donor to receive a stream of income on the donated assets during her lifetime plus the lifetime of either a spouse or a child. At the end of the life or lives, the principal amount still in the charitable annuity is gifted to a 501c(3) charitable organization. This can generate a substantial charitable deduction (although not 100% of the fair market value of the amount set aside for the annuity), and it reduces the estate tax obligation. In this case, the person who made the donation no longer owns the asset. Best of all, it creates a dependable stream of income for two joint lives. Unlike commercial annuities, no commissions are paid, so many people are not aware of them. If you are interested in this option, contact your local community foundation. For a national list, visit www.cof.org.

Another option is a donor-advised fund (DAF), a particularly effective vehicle when a large block of stock (e.g., employer stock) that has appreciated over a long period of time needs to be diversified. You can establish a DAF through a number of commercial custodians which offer this service (e.g., Schwab, Fidelity, and Vanguard) as well as many charitable religious, education, and community foundations. To open a DAF, you must contribute a minimum amount, generally $10,000 (but now there are several custodians who only require $5,000 to open the account). Your fund is professionally managed by the custodian that holds the account and grows tax free until it is used for grants to the charities that you nominate.

Charities must meet requirements of IRC 501c(3) to be eligible to receive grants (grants cannot be gifted to individuals). You cannot make grants from your DAF if you receive anything of value for the grant (e.g. charity auctions, dinners, raffle tickets, etc.). Also, you are eligible for a tax deduction for the contribution you make to your DAF in the year you contribute it, but you cannot take another charitable deduction when grants are made to charities from your DAF.

As a tax strategy, we recommend that whenever you are making a charitable donation of any sort, you transfer stocks or mutual funds which you have held for more than a year and have appreciated substantially. By transferring these assets, you avoid paying capital gains tax on the appreciation when sold, and you also receive a charitable deduction for the full market value of the asset when gifted.

A DAF makes it especially convenient to give to multiple charities. Without a DAF, if you wanted to gift highly appreciated stock to multiple charities, you would have to gift a portion of your shares to each charity. This means you would need multiple stock certificates issued or have each of the charities open an account at the brokerage firm where you hold the stock. With the DAF, you can make one contribution and direct the grants accordingly (as long as you meet the minimum grant requirement imposed by the public charity or foundation). Generally the minimum grant allowed is $250, but a number of custodians (including Fidelity, which is the largest) have lowered their minimum grants to $100. There are certain other complexities if contributions are made to DAFs in excess of 30% of your annual income, or if grants are to be made to certain types of private foundations, etc. Professional advice from disinterested counselors should be sought.

Sunset

Finally, the sunset stage comes when we have less than 12 months to live. Key at this stage is making sure that we have adequate cash flow to provide for continuing comfort in our last days. Paradoxically, this could mean impoverishing ourselves so we qualify for government aid for assisted living.

The rules regarding this stage of life change with regularity because the government has an interest in not allowing people to transfer their wealth to their heirs in order to become wards of the state. Government leaders want people to use their own resources before they rely on the government as a last resort. Congress has passed laws to invalidate transfers up to, at the current time, 60 months before being eligible for aid. Note that these rules may vary from state to state, depending on Medicaid laws.

Many of the people we see, however, feel that their health care and nursing home care are the responsibility of the government. They feel entitled to be taken care of in a reasonable fashion without having to impoverish themselves. Rather than having to use up the estate they have acquired, they want to pass the estate down to their children. Part of this is the concern of many people that if they are impoverished, their children will lose interest in their well-being.

> **Key at this stage is making sure that we have adequate cash flow to provide for continuing comfort in our last days.**

Various strategies can be utilized at this stage, all of which require the advice of specialists—elder care or elder law attorneys, AIDS patient attorneys, and other outside professionals whom financial advisors bring in as needed. One strategy, which has received a lot of press, is the *viatical settlement*, whereby an existing life insurance policy is liquidated by selling it to someone at a 25% to 50% discount off the face value to raise cash. In our experience, these arrangements tend to be fairly one-sided to the detriment of our clients. My general advice is to avoid viatical arrangements. If you find yourself in desperate need of the insurance proceeds, consult a reputable professional.

Keep in mind that death itself has certain tax and financial consequences. For example, capital assets such as stocks or real estate currently have the advantage of receiving a step-up in basis at death. This is more of my profession's jargon; all this means is that your heirs do not have to pay any tax on the accumulated capital gains your investments have generated in your lifetime. So if your parents bought their home 30 years ago for $50,000, and it's worth $750,000 when they die, you don't have to pay taxes on the $700,000 gain when you sell it. It is generally a mistake to sell assets like a house before death. It would make more sense to arrange a mortgage, or consider a "reverse mortgage." With a reverse mortgage, payments are made by the mortgage company to the owner of the home with the anticipation that on death of the owner, the home will be sold and the mortgage accumulated will be paid off. Reverse mortgages, however, are often touted by predatory financial advisors, and can involve a very high rate of interest, which is not obvious. It is wise get advice from a disinterested professional. Also, certain debts are automatically paid off or forgiven at death. Educational loans are paid off at death, as are loans at many credit unions. So it is ill-advised to pay off those kinds of debts in anticipation of impending death.

> A final consideration in the sunset stage is simplifying and consolidating your affairs to leave a hassle-free estate to your heirs.

A final consideration in the sunset stage is simplifying and consolidating your affairs to leave a hassle-free estate to your heirs. After 35 years of watching this process closely and helping people through it, I can tell you this is one of the most valuable legacies a person can leave. I have seen cases where people have been so into control that they made a complete mess of their estate by complicating the ownership interest in every asset. It was extremely difficult for the executors to untangle the web that had been constructed, and it ended up costing the estate far more in administrative expenses than the taxes the person was trying to avoid in the first place.

Functional Asset Allocation: A Simple, Sensible Strategy

> " The key to financial independence is knowing how much is enough. "
>
> —BERT WHITEHEAD

Earlier in this book, I said that investing is one of the easiest parts of my job. Helping people achieve and maintain their financial freedom isn't complicated. Then I said that for some reason almost everybody gets it wrong. People come to us with portfolios that have to be seen to be believed, and in long periods of a roaring bull market, many of them have managed to lose money every year.

This is not because they are stupid or unsuited to investing. It is because the financial environment in which we live fosters and encourages not just ignorance, but also misinformation about how to maintain a healthy, growing investment portfolio.

Even so-called experts who should know better seem to be contributing to the problem. Modern portfolio theory, on which most asset allocation theories are based, focuses on diversification across asset classes to reduce the risk in a portfolio. Usually, asset managers identify 6 to 12 different asset classes, and then they use computer models to ascertain the *efficient frontier*, that is, the exact mix of investments in each asset class that has historically provided the highest return for a given amount of risk.

One of the standard references that explains asset allocation and details the studies that support it is Roger Gibson's *Asset Allocation*. Some of the studies cited in that book have come under professional scrutiny and the conclusions may be open to question. Nonetheless, it is certainly a seminal work that is widely respected. A quick review of that book, however, confirms my premise that current asset allocation formulas used in our industry are not applicable to real people or to their assets.

In my real-world practice with people in various stages of financial development, I have become very skeptical of the precision and value of these computer models. As I mentioned earlier, although this approach seems to work for managing large pension funds, most people don't have enough zeros in their portfolio for it to work very well for them.

The much simpler approach I have developed for my clients is called Functional Asset Allocation. After 35 years of working with families and individuals as a financial advisor, I have found that each asset category serves an important function—a purpose—in people's lives. For example, although most money managers recognize real estate as a separate asset class, they do not consider it when constructing an asset allocation model. The value of your personal residence represents more than a straight financial calculation would indicate. As I said earlier, a great deal of your home's value is in your own enjoyment of it. That enjoyment can't be accounted for in fancy computer models. For professional money managers, it doesn't exist. It is also usually the largest and most profitable investment a family has. In our model, it is recognized as the best protection against inflation.

> I have found that each asset category serves an important function—a purpose—in people's lives.

Functional Asset Allocation is based on optimizing the way people utilize their assets in a household and on the psychological needs and life goals of real people in a dynamic society. Interestingly, our experience and comparative analysis have found that Functional Asset Allocation provides most of the benefits of diversification offered by modern portfolio theory. It also yields a better after-tax return with less risk for most of the people we work with.

THE THREE ASSET CATEGORIES OF FUNCTIONAL ASSET ALLOCATION

Functional Asset Allocation recognizes three main asset categories, and it distributes a client's assets across these three for specific purposes.

Interest Earning = Protection Against Deflation

The interest-earning asset category consists of two broad asset classes: cash and bonds. It serves the purpose of capital preservation. Regardless of what happens in the financial markets—and in people's lives—we want to make sure our clients have adequate cash flow in order to maintain their standard of living for a given period. Interest-earning investments protect you during deflation by providing a reliable cash flow while keeping this portion of your investment portfolio safe.

Real Estate = Protection Against Inflation

The real estate asset category is divided into three asset classes: personal residence, productive (including real estate investment, real estate investment trusts, and rental property), and nonproductive (such as vacant land, second homes, and passive limited partnerships). The unique functions of real estate include personal use and enjoyment and the opportunity to leverage your investment by mortgaging the property. Positive financial leverage through a home mortgage provides Americans with the most advantageous after-tax investment vehicle in the world.

Real estate investments offer protection during periods of inflation. Real estate is the most inflation-sensitive asset out there, although there is wide regional variation in housing appreciation. Leveraged real estate is the best inflation protection you can have if you have borrowed at a fixed rate of interest.

Equities = Profits During Prosperity

Equities are the growth engine of the portfolio but are also subject to the most volatility. Most standard asset allocation approaches ignore

The equities asset category includes four asset classes:

1. **Domestic equities**, which include mutual funds holding large company blue chip stocks as well as funds that hold stocks of smaller companies, which are more volatile but have greater growth potential.

2. **International funds and gold bullion**, which hedge the dollar,

3. Individual stock holdings, generally segregated because of the higher volatility with less diversification.

4. **Employer stock**, including outright purchases, grants, qualified and nonqualified options, as well as 401(k) matches, stock acquired from Employee Stock Purchase Plans (ESPPs), and Employee Stock Option Plan (ESOP) stock. (Various types of employer stock are segmented as a separate class because, for clients with generous employer plans, these holdings can be very large and impact diversification. Also the tax rules governing employer stock are very involved and must be taken into consideration when diversifying.)

the reality that company stock plans are the driving force (requiring careful tax management) in the portfolios of many employees. Reality requires that "recreational investments" in individual stocks, which involve ad hoc stock picking based on market timing systems and are comparable to gambling, carry a different risk component for small investors because there is not enough money to diversify adequately.

Equities provide growth during periods of prosperity. They are the engine that has enabled many families to greatly increase their net worth over the past decade.

The advantage of using the Functional Asset Allocation approach for your investment portfolio is that each asset class performs a discrete function within your portfolio. This enables you to hedge yourself against the two economic dangers, inflation and deflation, while still enabling you to have a part of your portfolio poised for growth in times of prosperity. This obviates the need for market timing. Firms that sell securities devised the traditional allocation systems used today by most financial advisors. Because they were devised by securities firms, they ignore important aspects of the portfolios of real people, such as their real estate holdings, complications involving employer stock, leverage, and tax considerations. These factors are not revenue producers for most financial advisory firms, so they are generally ignored by financial planners who work for financial institutions.

> Equities are the growth engine of the portfolio but are also subject to the most volatility.

THE ANALOGY OF THE FARMER

The most effective analogy I have found to help people understand Functional Asset Allocation is to think of your portfolio as if you were a farmer.

Your equities are the crops in your field. This is where you earn your livelihood. There needs to be some diversification. You may have corn, some wheat; you may even have some cows. You don't want to invest in only one crop. Not only would that increase the likelihood of being wiped out completely should insects or disease attack, but it would not be productive in the long term because consistently planting the same crop would deplete the soil of the nutrients necessary to help the crop grow. Depleted soil leads to a much lower yield. You also don't want to have too many different kinds of crops in your field because that would make it too difficult to farm efficiently.

Real estate is your garden. You have a house and a barn, some chickens and pigs running around, plus cucumbers and tomatoes growing. You are able to leverage the yield of your garden by using manure from the cows in the field for fertilizer and feeding some of your corn to the pigs.

Continued on next page

Your garden protects you against inflation. If the grocer in town were to raise food prices, you would be able to be self-sufficient by drawing from your garden. You also have flowers in your garden purely for personal enjoyment. This is the point: Your garden is not competing against your crops in the field for yield. They have two different purposes, two different functions. You wouldn't even think to compare the two.

Interest-earning investments can be compared to your pantry. As a prudent farmer, in good years you take some of your wheat and grind it into flour. You take some of the milk and churn it into butter and make it into cheese. Some of your beef is butchered and frozen. You draw from both your crops in the field and the surplus from your garden to fully stock your pantry. Farming is a volatile business, with many factors beyond your control—weather, disease, pestilence. You know you need to be able to sustain yourself through several years of drought if necessary. You stock your pantry so you can survive lean years (i.e., for capital preservation). Again, the point is that your pantry is not competing against your garden or your crops in the field for yield. It too has a completely different purpose, an independent function. When it comes to the pantry, safety trumps yield!

It can be difficult for clients to understand why bonds are important in their portfolio. Particularly in the 1990s with the raging bull market, inexperienced investors weren't interested in investments that, they said, "only" yielded 6% to 7%. With the abrupt beginning of the bear market in early 2000, the prudence of having a well-stocked pantry became apparent. Clients who had locked in long-term stripped Treasuries (more about this later) at 6% to 7% were well prepared for the market downturn. Those who only realized the need for capital appreciation after the market drop had to settle for Treasury bond yields of 4% to 5%.

THE CAMBRIDGE PYRAMID

To better understand the strategies that can be used to balance the pantry, the garden, and the crops in the field, I have designed a model shaped like a pyramid. Let's move on to some of the more technical aspects of understanding the function of investments.

The following explanation will be especially helpful if you want to learn more about investments and asset allocation. It will also appeal to you if you're already relatively astute about investments and would like to structure a fully functional investment portfolio.

An ordinary portfolio, which is at least 5 times the income of any household, becomes very powerful when it is designed around functionality. I have calculated that a portfolio modeled according to these principles has yielded 10% to 15% annually over any prior 15-year period since 1940. Focusing on functionality minimizes risk, enables perfect tax efficiency, and achieves consistently higher returns by fully utilizing the principles of modern portfolio theory.

As we look at Functional Asset Allocation in greater detail, let me share with you a graphic depiction that can make the whole concept easier to understand. I have called it the Cambridge Pyramid—the model we use in our work to display and track asset allocation and portfolio growth for our own clients (see Figure 8.1). Most of our clients have found this snapshot of their financial net worth to be far more understandable than the traditional accountants' balance sheet with long lists of numbers. Let's first look at how the pyramid is built, one level at a time.

> **Focusing on functionality minimizes risk, enables perfect tax efficiency, and achieves consistently higher returns.**

The A Level of the Pyramid

Each block in the pyramid is made up of investments in various asset classes (see Figure 8.2). The A level is the foundation of the pyramid. If you remember the building the foundation stage of the Financial Life Cycle, this level corresponds to the five fundamentals of fiscal fitness.

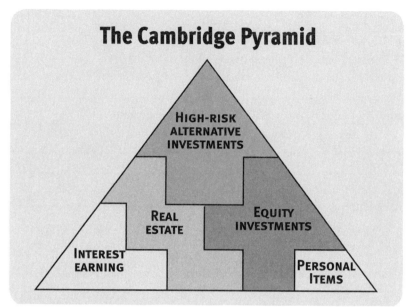

The Cambridge Pyramid

HIGH-RISK ALTERNATIVE INVESTMENTS

REAL ESTATE

EQUITY INVESTMENTS

INTEREST EARNING

PERSONAL ITEMS

FIGURE 8.1

A-1. Cash and Cash Equivalents. Includes CDs, money markets, savings and checking accounts, and so on, that are tied up for less than 18 months. Typically, the interest rates on these investments can change, but the principal you have invested is not at risk due to market changes. This represents your cash reserves.

A-2. Emergency Cash Equivalents. Encompasses all tax-advantaged cash equivalents, such as U.S. savings bonds, the cash value of life insurance policies, IRAs or other retirement funds invested in CDs or money markets. Like A-1, the interest rate may change, but the principal is not at risk. A-2 is your emergency cash. A-1 plus A-2 equals your total liquidity reserves.

A-3. Personal Residence. Equity (fair market value minus mortgage) in your home. So, for example, if the fair market value of your home is $250,000 and your mortgage balance is $200,000, then the equity in your home is $50,000.

A-4. Employer Stock. Stock in a publicly traded company where you are employed. This includes the net value of both qualified and nonqualified stock options that are vested, as well as restricted stock,

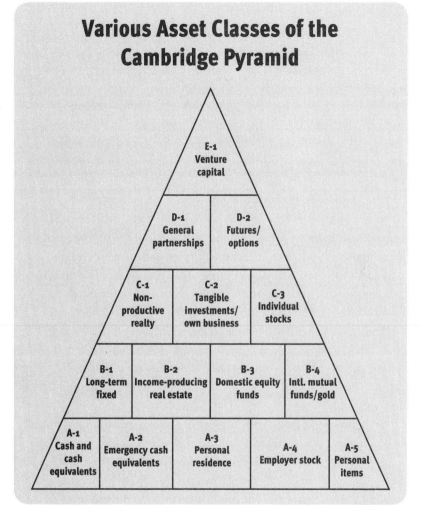

Various Asset Classes of the Cambridge Pyramid

E-1
Venture capital

D-1
General partnerships

D-2
Futures/options

C-1
Non-productive realty

C-2
Tangible investments/own business

C-3
Individual stocks

B-1
Long-term fixed

B-2
Income-producing real estate

B-3
Domestic equity funds

B-4
Intl. mutual funds/gold

A-1
Cash and cash equivalents

A-2
Emergency cash equivalents

A-3
Personal residence

A-4
Employer stock

A-5
Personal items

FIGURE 8.2

stock purchased through ESOP and ESPP programs, company matching stock in 401(k)s, stock grants, and stock purchased on the open market.

A-5. Personal Items. Includes cars, furniture, boats, toys, and so on. The value of everything in this block of the pyramid is the fair market value of assets that are depreciating, less any consumer debt.

The B Level of the Pyramid

The B level represents the diversification of investments.

B-1. Long-Term Fixed Investments. Investments that earn interest and are tied up for longer than 18 months, including bonds, bond mutual funds, promissory notes, mortgages or land contracts that represent money owed to you by others and that have a fixed rate of interest. The value of these assets fluctuates inversely to interest rates, meaning that if interest rates go up, the value of these assets goes down, and vice versa.

B-2. Income-Producing Real Estate. Equity in real estate that produces income, such as rental houses, real estate mutual funds, commercial property leased out, as well as property in shared equity arrangements, and so on. Shared equity arrangements involve partnerships where one party (usually the parent) makes the down payment for the other partner (usually the child) to enable the child to buy a home. The child qualifies for the mortgage, makes the payments, and lives in the home. After a period of time, usually 5 years, the home is sold and the parent gets his or her money back plus half of the profit on the home. The child takes the rest of the money to make a down payment on a home, which the child can buy on his or her own then.

B-3. Domestic Equity Funds. Domestic equity mutual funds typically hold stocks in large and small U.S. companies.

B-4. International Mutual Funds/Gold Bullion Coins. These investments hedge the dollar; in other words, when the U.S. dollar loses value relative to other currencies or to gold, these investments increase in value, so they protect the investor against domestic inflation. We include most global funds here as well.

The C Level of the Pyramid

The C level represents investments that are generally less desirable, due to higher risk, higher transaction and carrying costs, and illiquidity.

C-1. Nonproductive Realty. Real estate limited partnerships, vacation homes, timeshares and vacant land. They are easy to buy, hard to sell.

C-2. Tangible Investments/Own Business. Oil and gas limited partnerships, jewelry, antiques, collectibles, and investment-grade art. Also, the equity (if unknown, the book value) of closely held businesses, because they are very difficult to market. These investments are especially risky because there is typically a huge spread between bid and asked prices (i.e., wholesale vs. retail).

C-3. Individual Stocks. On the C level because of their volatility. Most small investors don't have enough money to buy a sufficient number of individual stocks to diversify their equities properly. For investors who have a large enough portfolio (over $1 million) to diversify properly using individual stocks, I use B-3 for large cap domestic stocks and C-3 for small cap stocks (described below).

The D Level of the Pyramid

These kinds of investments are usually not available to the public, but are private placements with high minimums and often-prohibitive costs, such as hedge funds, which are very risky, unregulated funds that deal in very esoteric financial strategies involving derivatives, collateralized obligations, option collars, etc. They require a level of sophistication that most people don't have, and carry "suitability requirements" detailing how much an investor's net worth is. They are very illiquid (i.e., hard to convert back to cash) and require long holding periods, without giving investors any control over the investment. Because of the high level of volatility of these investments, most people don't have any business playing around on the D and E levels. Each level in the Cambridge pyramid represents investments that have more risk that those on the next level down.

D-1. General Partnerships/Entertainment and Sports Investments. Racehorses, sports teams, and other off-the-wall investments.

D-2. Leveraged and Margined Investments. Highly leveraged commodity deals, such as buying pork bellies on margin, currency speculation, options, futures, and so on. A hallmark of these investments is that borrowed money is used to finance the investment, or options are bought which have no intrinsic value to speculate on price movements in the financial markets.

The E Level of the Pyramid

E-1. Venture Capital. Money given to others to start their own business.

When people come to us, we take a complete inventory of their assets and investments. We then categorize and display them on the Cambridge Pyramid before we begin discussing asset allocation or investment strategy. First we look at how well the foundation is built. If the foundation is not solid, those issues must be addressed first. Once the foundation is solid, we can concentrate on Functional Asset Allocation—the balance among interest-earning investments, real estate, and equities.

STRUCTURING A PORTFOLIO USING FUNCTIONAL ASSET ALLOCATION

Asset allocation refers to balancing the types of investments in your portfolio, including real estate, interest earning (bonds and cash), and equities (stocks). It is tempting, as some advisors suggest, to shift assets around and rebalance to "time the market."

Market timing is so prevalent a dysfunction that it deserves mention at the outset of our discussion of asset allocation. Trying to time the market involves predicting how much investments, such as stocks, will sell for in the near future. This may be within a day (called *day trading*), or over a few weeks or even several months. All of these are considered short-term periods in investing.

Timing can be based on a number of different exogenous factors, such as financial ratios (for example, a company's price/earnings ratio) or speculation as to where interest rates are going. Different analysts use different criteria for their predictions, so there is never complete consensus on where the market is headed.

Market timing has always been a failed strategy. Of the thousands of studies conducted by pension companies, academics, and independent experts, never has a single study found that any market timing system works in the long term, nor even consistently in the short term. It is only those sectors of the financial industry that earn revenue when their customers engage in frequent trading—such as wirehouses, investment newsletters, TV shows, and so forth—that espouse timing schemes.

> **Market timing has always been a failed strategy.**

Consider this illustration. Assume Tim invests $1,000 into the market at the lowest point of each year for 20 years. Assume Rosario puts $1,000 into the market buying the same stocks as Tim, but invests at the highest point every year for 20 years. The result after 20 years: Tim has an annual return of 11.8%; Rosario's return is 11.4%. The difference in the performance of their portfolios is statistically negligible.

If you attempt to time the market, you'll have to make two decisions correctly: first, when to sell; then, when to buy back in. It is difficult enough to make one of those decisions correctly, much less both of them. The above example assumes that Tim did it right every single year, which is well nigh impossible. More often than not, market timers make less on their investments than people who invest regularly and hold on to their investments. Investing your money based on your life situation, the endogenous approach we discussed earlier, means your buying decisions are determined by your personal goals and your investments are made for the long term.

Sometimes people will ask me, "Where do you think the market is headed, Bert?" My response is always, "Well they took a poll yesterday of all the 'smart money' traders, and exactly half thought the market was going up and half thought it was going down!" This is the stark reality: *For every buyer there must be a seller—and one of them is wrong!*

It is this interplay of buying and selling that determines the price of a stock. So at any price, by definition, half the "smart money" thinks a stock is going to go up and half thinks it is going to go down.

True asset allocation is not a market timing approach. It is based on holding investments for the long term in certain proportions that create a balanced portfolio. With a balanced portfolio, there will always be some investment in the portfolio going down, but those losses are offset, or "hedged," by other investments that are gaining value at the same time. Altogether, this mix of investments will appreciate overall with less risk and will produce a higher rate of return than trading based on speculation. This is the basis of modern portfolio theory.

> **This is the stark reality: For every buyer there must be a seller—and one of them is wrong!**

Most asset allocation models focus only on stocks and bonds, since the financial industry makes most of its profits from these categories of investments. Functional Asset Allocation includes real estate as a separate asset category that must figure in the balancing equation. Real estate is an important part of most families' financial plan, because their home is typically their largest investment, and usually the one they make the most profit on.

Note that this idea of using the three categories of stocks, bonds, and real estate in asset allocation is not new. The first written asset allocation formula was in the Talmud, written over 2,000 years ago. It exhorts investors to "invest a third in land, a third in business, and a third in reserves." Functional Asset Allocation over the long term approaches precisely that balance of investments. Here are the directions for achieving the right balance in your portfolio.

Real Estate

When initially structuring or rebalancing a portfolio, always start with real estate. This is because real estate is the most illiquid of investments. The rest of the portfolio should take into account the issues and opportunities that real estate provides.

For example, if a portfolio is heavily overweighted in leveraged real estate, the client owns too much real estate in relation to other investments, and the real estate is heavily mortgaged. Then it is critical to reduce the risk of the remainder of the investments and provide extra liquidity until the real estate overhang can be corrected. Sometimes a client's real estate is a loafing asset, which means it does not have enough of a mortgage. The mortgage is referred to as a leverage. In real estate investing, leverage means the amount of loans made with the home or other real estate pledged as collateral, i.e., the mortgage. Since the real estate will appreciate the same amount whether it is fully leveraged or not, often it is advisable to remortgage, which would enable the home owner to pull out cash to better diversify other investments.

As you have read several times in this book, most people make more money on their real estate than on any other single investment. This is particularly true of the single-family home used as a primary residence. In addition, the positive financial leverage created by a fixed-rate home mortgage gives Americans the most advantageous after-tax investment vehicle in the world.

The function of real estate is to protect against inflation and provide personal enjoyment. Positive financial leverage is created when you borrow money at one rate of interest and invest that money at a higher rate of interest. The fixed-rate home mortgage is one of the best examples of positive financial leverage. We tend to take it for granted, but in fact no other country in the world allows its citizens to borrow large sums of money (relative to income) at a fixed rate of interest over such a long period.

> **When initially structuring or rebalancing a portfolio, always start with real estate.**

Inflation is the loss of purchasing power through a general rise in prices. During periods of inflation, a debtor repays loans (such as a mortgage) with dollars that are worth less in purchasing power than the dollars originally borrowed. Locking in a fixed-rate mortgage protects the purchasing power of your housing dollars, creating a buffer against inflation.

A study conducted in 1978 found that not only is real estate a hedge against inflation, but that leveraged private residential real estate is the only investment that offers complete protection against inflation. That is because when there is inflation, the interest yield on investments increases while the rate of fixed-rate mortgages remains the same. Not only are you achieving "positive leverage" because your money is earning more than the funds you have invested are costing you, but you also are repaying the mortgage in cheaper dollars.

Inflation can be either anticipated or unanticipated. Investments that offer protection against anticipated inflation, such as debt instruments whose yields adjust for the anticipated inflation rate, offer no protection against unanticipated inflation. Private residential real estate, however, protects against both.

Beware, however, of financial sales reps who suggest borrowing money on your house to invest in life insurance or annuities. The commissions you'll be paying more than wipe out any advantage you could derive from the mortgage.

> **Locking in a fixed-rate mortgage protects the purchasing power of your housing dollars, creating a buffer against inflation.**

There are three key steps to properly allocating real estate assets under Functional Asset Allocation. First is having the appropriate percentage of assets invested in real estate. Second is having those real estate assets properly leveraged. Third is properly buttressing real estate debt with liquidity.

In looking at the appropriate percentage of assets to invest in real estate, we must first define our terms. Most of the people who visit our offices are familiar with what is meant by the term *net worth*—total assets (everything you own) minus liabilities (everything you owe). However, when determining asset allocation percentages, net worth becomes an inaccurate measure. This is because *net worth* includes assets that are either not readily marketable (such as jewelry or art) or are not true investments (such as cars and boats).

So instead of net worth, we focus on marketable assets when determining appropriate asset balance in a portfolio. On the Cambridge Pyramid, marketable assets are represented in Figure 8.3 by the assets held in the blocks outlined with a dotted line. Net marketable assets include only the equity in investments (the number excludes mortgages; student loans; and margin loans, or loans against stock holdings). Total marketable assets represent the fair market value of all the investments included without netting out associated debt.

Appropriate Percentage of Assets in Real Estate. Functional Asset Allocation calls for 25% to 40% of total marketable assets to be held in real estate. For those who are real estate professionals or who own commercial property, this percentage may be increased to 30% to 60% of total marketable assets.

Proper Leverage of Real Estate Assets. Functional Asset Allocation calls for 50% to 80% leverage on real estate assets. So if your home were worth $200,000, a mortgage of $100,000 (50%) to $160,000 (80%) would be appropriate for real estate investors, the proper leverage range is 30% to 60%. As mentioned earlier, this leverage provides a long-term investment advantage and an additional buffer against inflation.

Adequate Liquidity to Support Mortgage Debt. Functional Asset Allocation also requires a person in good financial shape to have adequate liquidity to support the mortgage debt load he's carrying.

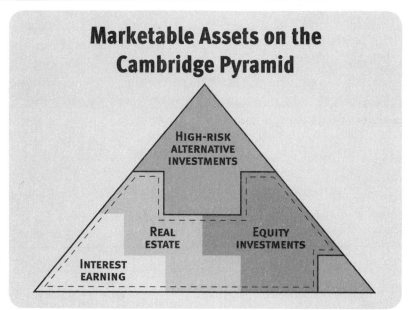

Marketable Assets on the Cambridge Pyramid

HIGH-RISK ALTERNATIVE INVESTMENTS

REAL ESTATE

EQUITY INVESTMENTS

INTEREST EARNING

FIGURE 8.3

We have previously discussed liquidity needs as a percentage of income; an employed individual requires 10% of his annual income in cash reserves (Box A-1 on the Cambridge Pyramid) and twice that amount as emergency liquidity (Box A-2).

In our offices, we apply a second liquidity test: An amount equal to 20% of outstanding mortgages should be kept in liquid assets (Boxes A-1 and A-2). If these two tests produce different results, we select the greater number as the adequate liquidity amount. Keeping at least 20% of outstanding mortgages in liquid assets ensures that you will be able to continue paying your mortgage for 2 years, even if your income abruptly stops.

For most people with a properly constructed pyramid, the numbers returned should balance out quite easily.

To illustrate: Tom and Brenda earn $100,000 a year and have an investment portfolio of $200,000. To properly build the foundation of their pyramid, they keep 10%, or $10,000, in their money market account (A-1). They keep twice that amount, or $20,000, in U.S. savings bonds as their emergency liquidity, for a total liquidity package of $30,000. They have $100,000 invested in their 401(k) plans, all in stock mutual funds. They have another $70,000 invested in individual stocks through a retail brokerage account. They recently purchased a home valued at $225,000, putting 20% down and securing a mortgage of $180,000. Page 179 shows how we would evaluate the real estate portion of Tom and Brenda's portfolio.

To evaluate the real estate portion of their portfolio, we apply the following tests:

1. What percentage of their total marketable assets is held in real estate? Their total marketable assets are $425,000; the real estate portion of that is $225,000, representing 53%. This exceeds the recommended guidelines of 20% to 40%. Thus they should not buy more real estate until they have accumulated more stocks, bonds, and cash.

2. How does the value of their home relate to their annual income? With an annual income of $100,000 and a home valued at $225,000, their home is 2.25 times their annual income. This is within the recommended guidelines of 2 to 2.5 times. So they are neither overhoused nor underhoused.

3. Is their real estate properly leveraged? Their home is leveraged 80%, within the recommended guidelines of 50% to 80%. This provides adequate protection against inflation.

4. Do they have sufficient liquidity? To meet the five fundamentals test of liquidity, they need to have 10% of their income in the A-1 level, in cash and cash-equivalent assets, and twice that amount in A-2 assets. Their $30,000 fulfills this requirement. But the second test that must be applied is whether they have 20% of their outstanding mortgages in liquid assets. Twenty percent of $180,000 is $36,000, meaning Tom and Brenda need to increase their liquid assets by $6,000. This would ensure they could support the leverage in their portfolio.

The two issues—too high a percentage of their portfolio in real estate and insufficient liquidity—will need to be addressed when devising an appropriate investment strategy for Tom and Brenda. Before we can formulate recommendations that will boost their financial fitness, we also have to factor in their stage in the Financial Life Cycle, their personal investment horizon, their family values and goals, and the amount of risk exposure appropriate to their situation.

Although the personal residence usually represents the biggest chunk of the real estate portion of the portfolio, other kinds of real estate investments are available as well. These include second homes, vacation homes, real estate investment trusts (REITs), rental homes, vacant land, and passive limited partnerships. These other real estate investments can represent opportunities for geographic diversification, which is the biggest challenge when working with the real estate portion of the portfolio. When property values in California are increasing, property values in Michigan may be dropping. Even within a state, there are regional variations, so property in San Diego could be rapidly rising in price while property in Sacramento may be appreciating much more slowly. These real estate investment alternatives also present their own unique risks, which make them inappropriate for most investors. Once real estate is evaluated, we move on to the interest-earning portion of the portfolio.

Interest-Earning Portion of Portfolio

The interest-earning category is divided into three asset classes: cash and cash equivalents (maturing in less than 18 months), tax-sheltered cash equivalents, and bonds (maturing in 18 months to 30 years). The function of interest-earning investments is capital preservation and deflation protection.

You don't read much about deflation, but those of us in the financial field are very concerned about it. In fact, we are worried that it will become the next financial crisis our clients will have to deal with. *Deflation* occurs when the level of economic activity is decreasing, as when we are in a recession or depression. Generally, during periods of deflation companies lay off workers; as a result, unemployment rises, wages stagnate or maybe even drop, and both interest rates and corporate profits decline.

The devastating aspect of deflation is that it happens very suddenly. Inflation tends to warm up and then pick up speed, so we have a little time to prepare for it. But deflation hits before you have a chance to react. The last serious round of deflation in the United States was the Great Depression. Japan, however, has been dealing with severe deflation for more than 10 years. The Nikkei Index dropped from just under 40,000 to 24,000 in 1999 and then lost half again in value in the following 18 months. Since then it has fluctuated between 10,000 and 20,000 during the past decade.

Keep in mind that Japan is not just a developing nation; it is the world's second largest industrial economy.

If we were to replicate the deflation in Japan here in the United States, we would be looking at these alarming possibilities:

1. A stock market drop of 60%, bringing the Dow to under 5,000
2. The collapse of the real estate market, with homes selling at less than half of what they sell for now—if they sell at all
3. Interest rates dropping to 1%

Most people don't stay up nights worrying about this, but in our field it is folly to disregard the potential for worldwide financial disruption. After all, our money is basically just pictures of dead presidents. Because the dollar is not backed by gold or other hard assets, its value depends completely on our faith in the system. Our own history, as well as the Asian experience, has shown how quickly that confidence can evaporate.

Functional Asset Allocation addresses this risk as well as we believe it can be addressed. It is very common for us to see clients in the accumulation stages become impatient with the return on their interest-earning investments as compared to their equity investments (at least during a bull market). It's understandably frustrating to see assets earning 5% to 7% when the stock market is returning 15% to 20%. But one of the basic tenets of Functional Asset Allocation is that the three asset categories do not compete with each other for yield. Rather, they each serve a specific function. Should the time come that we experience a severe deflation environment, the interest-earning assets will be the heroes of the portfolio.

Interest-earning investments carry two types of risk: the risk of default (i.e., the issuer will go bankrupt) and interest rate risk. The value of bonds decreases when interest rates rise. For instance, if you invest in a $10,000 bond at 7% and interest rates increase to 9%, you will not be able to sell your bond for the $10,000 you paid (although you will get the full $10,000 back when the bond matures, if the issuer does not go broke). The loss from selling your bond after rates go up is called a *discount*.

Conversely, if interest rates drop after you buy a bond, you could sell it for a profit (before it matures), which is called a *premium*. Because of this additional risk, usually bonds pay more interest (a higher yield) than cash.

The advantage of cash equivalents is that they are *liquid*, which means they can be converted to cash quickly without risk of loss of capital. This is why money market accounts and short-term CDs pay a lower yield than longer-term bonds and CDs.

Bonds are *marketable*, which means they can be converted to cash quickly, but there is a risk of loss if interest rates have risen since the purchase of the bond or the issuer has become insolvent. Bonds are the best way to guard against deflation, because, unlike stocks, they provide a fixed rate of interest over a long period of time as well as the promise of a full return of your investment.

Corporations as well as municipalities and the U.S. Treasury issue bonds. Corporate bonds have the best yield (i.e., interest as a percentage of your investment), and *junk bonds*, which are issued by companies with impaired credit ratings, have the highest yields of all. Municipal bonds have the advantage of being exempt from federal tax as well as state tax in the state of issue. This tax advantage is factored into their yield, which is lower than that of other bonds.

We usually recommend U.S. Treasury bonds. Although these have a lower yield, the interest is exempt from state taxes. The reason the yield is so low is simply because they are absolutely the safest investment in the world. The U.S. government could default, but if it does, it is likely to be the last one to go under.

Another very significant advantage to U.S. Treasury bonds is they are *noncallable*. Corporate and municipal bonds have a provision that the issuer can pay off the bonds early and buy them back. So if interest rates drop, they just issue a new round of bonds at the lower rate and then pay off their outstanding bonds—saving them the cost of having to pay higher-than-market rates for the rest of the term of the bond. Therefore, if you buy a 20-year corporate bond with a 9% yield, you don't have a guarantee that you will get that rate for the whole 20 years. You can bet that if rates drop to 4% to 6%, your bond will be called. By contrast, with a U.S. Treasury bond, the interest rate is guaranteed at the time the bond is issued and it cannot be paid off early.

> **Bonds are the best way to guard against deflation, because, unlike stocks, they provide a fixed rate of interest over a long period of time.**

When allocating interest-earning funds between short term (A-1 and A-2) and long term (B-1), our basic recommendation is to allocate a minimum of 25% each (assuming all basic liquidity requirements have been met). The remaining 50% "swing" can then be designated short term or long term based on your liquidity needs. Normally in the Foundation and Early Accumulation stages of the financial life cycle, short term interest earning investments (A-1 and A-2) will be predominant. Later in life, bonds (B-1) will gradually increase to 75%.

Capital preservation is vital in all stages of the Financial Life Cycle, but it becomes extremely important during the conservation and largess stages. Clients tell us that their main concern in retirement is to make sure they don't run out of money. This is the reason many people avoid investing in the stock market after they quit working.

A primary strategy we use during these stages is the building of a bond ladder. In brief, a bond ladder uses bonds (preferably stripped Treasuries, which we'll discuss shortly) purchased with sequential maturities so a different bond matures every year.

How Bond Ladders Work

Bond ladders are one of the most popular investment approaches we use with clients approaching retirement. Let's discuss how this strategy works, its advantages and disadvantages, and alternatives when it is not appropriate from a tax standpoint.

First, an explanation of laddered stripped Treasuries may be helpful. Treasuries are IOUs (i.e., bonds, notes, and bills) issued by the U.S. government. They are globally traded and, as discussed, are considered the safest investment in the world, which is why they carry a very low rate of interest relative to other bonds. They are available with maturities of one month to 30 years, and they normally pay out interest every 6 months. Denominations generally are available in $1,000 increments, starting at $10,000.

Stripped Treasuries are Treasury securities that pay out no interest but are sold at a discount from their face value and at maturity can be cashed in at face value. This type of bond is sometimes called a *zero-coupon bond*. In effect, the interest earned is reinvested instead of paid out. The advantage of this is that the interest doesn't have to be reinvested every 6 months, but it automatically earns the rate of the original bond.

For example, assume that the long bonds (i.e., 30-year Treasury bonds) are paying just over 6% interest per year. Shorter-term bonds usually pay a somewhat lower rate of interest. For the sake of our example, assume that 12-year bonds are paying exactly 6%. (The yield curve is very flat normally from 10 years to 30 years without much increase in the yield. Most of the increase is usually between one year and 10, although at times there is an anomaly called an "inverted yield curve," in which some short-term rates are actually higher than long-term rates. This has often been a harbinger of recession.) Therefore, if you bought a regular 12-year Treasury bond for $10,000, you would get $300 interest paid to you every 6 months (or $600 per year).

Because money invested at 6% doubles in 12 years, due to compounding, instead of buying a regular 12-year Treasury bond for $10,000, you could buy a stripped Treasury with a face value of $20,000 due 12 years from now for the same $10,000. Although no interest will be paid, the discount when you purchase the bond ensures that you will earn a 6% compounded rate for the life of the bond. When the bond matures, it will be worth $20,000 because the interest accrued over the 12 years has been reinvested.

> A *bond ladder* refers to a series of bonds bought with sequential maturities, so a bond matures every year.

A *bond ladder* refers to a series of bonds bought with sequential maturities, so a bond matures every year. Laddering stripped Treasuries provides a cash flow guaranteed by the U.S. government.

In designing portfolios for clients approaching retirement, the clincher to providing them with peace of mind is to make sure they will not run out of money. So we have to determine how much they need to live on per year and how much of this will come from pensions and Social Security. The rest can be guaranteed by using strips as part of a diversified portfolio.

For example, if a client needs $80,000 a year to live on, and pension and Social Security payments will contribute $35,000, we want to have a 15-year ladder built by the time he retires that provides $45,000 a year. At current interest rates, if the ladder starts in 2 to 3 years, it will take about $450,000 to invest in the ladder today to provide this cash flow. This usually amounts to 50% to 60% of a client's investment portfolio, and the balance can provide liquidity and can be invested in the stock market.

If you want to fully fund a bond ladder, Exercise 8.1, "Funding a

Funding a Bond Ladder

Expenses per year in retirement: $_____

Minus Social Security income: $_____

Minus pension income: $_____

= Annual cash flow needed
from bond ladder: $_____

                                         × 10

Approximate amount needed to
fund 15-year bond ladder fully: $_____

EXERCISE 8.1

Bond Ladder," calculates approximately how much it would cost.

This combination of supersafe bonds and a well-diversified stock portfolio has averaged a combined return of about 8% to 9% over the past 70 years. What's key is that now the client has locked in an assured investment horizon of 15 years. The ladder will be replenished during the period when the stock market is good. Because the bonds are guaranteeing 5% to 6%, as long as the stock market earns more than 5% a year on average over the 15-year period, the client will never run out of money.

Each year we determine whether to withdraw the funds provided from the bonds maturing in the ladder or to take capital gains from the stock market. In good years, the funds coming from the ladder are reinvested at the long end of the ladder, where they will generally buy 2 years for every year that matures. When the stock market is weak, the cash flow provided from the ladder is used for living expenses instead of selling stock. This ensures that the stocks in the portfolio are always bought low and sold high.

The critical part of this strategy is to make a bond ladder tax-efficient. The best way to invest money that is in a qualified pension plan (e.g., IRA) is in the stripped Treasury ladder. This ensures that the interest will accumulate on a tax-deferred basis, and also that adequate funds will be available for minimum withdrawals when required.

If a client does not have adequate funds in qualified plans to build the total ladder, we can use insured municipal bonds up to 10 years out, because many noncallable municipal bonds are available for that short a maturity. Likewise, we often recommend FDIC-insured CDs for the first 5 years, rather than Treasuries because they carry the same government guarantee, are noncallable, and pay a slightly higher yield because they are not negotiable.

> We usually like to start building a client's ladder when she starts planning for the financial independence stage.

We usually like to start building a client's ladder when she starts planning for the financial independence stage. At this point her marketable net worth should be 7 to 10 times her annual living expenses. At this stage, we start with a ladder as small as 50% of her projected cash flow needs for as little as 5 years out—starting with the year she plans to stop working full time. Each year we grow the ladder so we have at least 7 years fully funded when the client may be dependent on it, and continue to grow the ladder so there are 15 years funded when the client stops working entirely.

Over the years, this Cambridge strategy has proven to protect our clients in the most financially vulnerable part of their lives while giving them the peace of mind to enjoy their golden years.

Equities

Equities are the growth engine that drives the portfolio. Historically, the stock market has increased 11% a year over the last 70 years. That doesn't mean stocks go up every year. If you have a long investment horizon, however, you can be pretty much assured that over a period of 10 to 15 years the stock market will go up.

Some financial advisors, particularly inexperienced advisors or those working for companies performing research and analysis, tend to want to divide equities into numerous categories. These categories include large cap, mid cap, small cap, value, growth, and so on. Morningstar is a well-known independent investment rating service. The typical Morningstar approach results in nine categories just for U.S. stocks and another nine for international stocks, which are then frequently subdivided further by regional concentration. (Interest-earning investments are similarly categorized as high risk, medium risk, low risk, short term, long term, intermediate term, etc.)

Paying attention to all these fine divisions and distinctions may make sense if you happen to be managing a $20 billion pension account, but most of the people we work with simply do not have enough zeros in their portfolios to worry about all this. In our practice, we identify three broad asset classes among equity investments: large cap, small cap, and international (we'll discuss each of these in detail shortly). I believe these are functionally distinct. Large cap stocks are traded in a very efficient market; the small cap stock market is relatively inefficient; international stocks offer a hedge against the dollar.

> **If you have a long investment horizon, you can be pretty much assured that over a period of 10 to 15 years the stock market will go up.**

First let's discuss *market efficiency*. It's easy to understand the efficiency of markets by comparing the stock market with real estate. Real estate is one of the best examples of an inefficient market. No two pieces of real estate are the same. Virtually everyone in the real estate market (especially the single-family residence market) is an inexperienced buyer or seller because they only buy or sell a house once every 10 or 20 years (sometimes only once in a lifetime!).

So in real estate you can find good deals. You can find houses priced too low for the market if you are willing to take the time to hunt around. Compare this with the stock market. Every single share of GM common stock is exactly the same as every other. The people who trade stocks often trade them on a daily basis. Stocks are sold and resold constantly. If you are hunting for GM stock, you can hunt all you want but you are not going to find a better deal on GM stock than someone else at the same time, because it's too efficient a market.

Large Cap Stocks

Large capitalization stocks are those of large companies that have more than a billion dollars worth of total capitalization (i.e., price per share times the number of shares outstanding). These represent the 2,000 to 3,000 largest corporations in America, and as such are the most closely scrutinized investments in the world. The market for large cap stocks is ruthlessly efficient.

Consider these factors: A limited number of these companies exist. Their information is always publicly available. Not only is the information disclosed, but it is also widely disseminated over the Internet. New information is factored instantly into the price of these securities. Tens of thousands, if not hundreds of thousands, of people study them every day. They are traded in the millions of shares.

These factors are the classic hallmarks of an efficient market. All of which means it is virtually impossible for any single individual investor to be able to outperform the market over a long period by trying to pick large cap stocks.

It is rare even for a money manager to add value to a portfolio by selecting any combination of large cap stocks, since all information relative to the stock is already reflected in the price. In fact, studies have shown that large cap index funds (see below) outperform, on average, 85% of managed funds. Some years that figure may be as high as 90% to 95%. In other years it may drop to 70% to 75%, but the fact is that the vast majority of money managers cannot beat large cap index funds consistently.

Certainly there are rare exceptions. When Peter Lynch ran the Fidelity Magellan Fund, he ran up an astonishing record of out-performing the S&P 500 for 15 years. But this is again a function of the law of large numbers, not a reflection of superior stock-picking ability. In any random distribution, there will inevitably be abnormal occurrences at the ends of the bell curve. These exceptions indeed prove the rule. Peter Lynch, legend though he may be, was not a guru;

> **Buying mutual funds enables smaller investors to get critical diversification.**

while he was very savvy, his outstanding record was primarily due to luck.

Unless a client's investment portfolio exceeds $1 million, I recommend that she use mutual funds instead of buying individual stocks and bonds. The reason is that, with less than $1 million, an investor doesn't have enough money to buy enough different stocks in large enough blocks to be economical. Buying mutual funds enables smaller investors to get critical diversification. To be diversified, a portfolio should have at least 50 individual stocks in each asset category (for example a minimum of 50 large companies, 50 small companies, etc.). Without this diversification, the portfolio will be extremely volatile and hence much more risky. Mutual funds aggregate investments from many investors in a pool and invest in a large number of stocks or bonds. If a manager is hired to pick stocks, the fund is considered "actively managed." Now, however, "passive investments" are very popular. These mutual funds are called *index funds*.

An index fund is a group of stocks selected to mirror a particular index. The most common large cap index is the S&P 500. Others include the NASDAQ 100 (the largest 100 stocks on the NASDAQ), the Dow Jones (the 30 stocks that comprise the Dow Jones Industrial Average), and the Wilshire 5000 Index (a total market index).

Index funds have three main advantages over managed funds

1. They outperform managed funds the vast majority of the time, as noted earlier.

2. In general they are very low cost. All mutual funds have administration expenses that are passed on to the shareholders and expressed as an expense ratio, expressed in turn as a number of basis points. (*Basis point* is a financial term

meaning .01%; one hundred basis points equal 1%.) The Vanguard Index 500, for example, has an expense ratio of only 22 to 24 *basis points*, or 0.22% to 0.24%. Over time, paying 20 basis points as opposed to 100 basis points makes a phenomenal difference in the amount of money you can accumulate (see Figure 8.4). Exchange-traded funds (ETFs)—essentially index funds traded on the stock exchange—have even lower expenses, in the range of only 12 to 18 basis points. These include Diamonds (symbol = DIA, based on the Dow Jones), Cubes (symbol = QQQ, based on the NASDAQ 100), and Spyders (symbol SPY, based on the S&P 500).

3. Index funds generally are very tax-efficient. In a managed mutual fund, the fund manager makes decisions during the year about which stocks to buy or sell. A typical large cap managed fund has a turnover of 100% or greater, meaning that, on average, every stock in the portfolio is sold once a year. When these stocks are sold, the gains and losses are netted against each other. If the fund ends up with a net trading loss for the year, it is carried over to the next year. Under current tax law if the fund has a gain for the year, the gain must be distributed to the shareholders, who are taxed on it as a long-term capital gain distribution. This is in addition to the taxable income they receive as their share of the dividends as owners of the mutual fund. ETFs are even more tax-efficient than index funds, since capital gains are not distributed or taxed each year, but only when you choose to sell the fund.

Index funds, however, do very little trading—only when stocks are added to or subtracted from the index on which they are based. So instead of 100% turnover, they may have only 1% (e.g., the Schwab 1000, managed for tax efficiency) to 6% (e.g., the Vanguard S&P 500) turnover. Thus on an annual basis, virtually the only tax the shareholder is required to pay is on the dividends that are generated, typically 1% of total asset value.

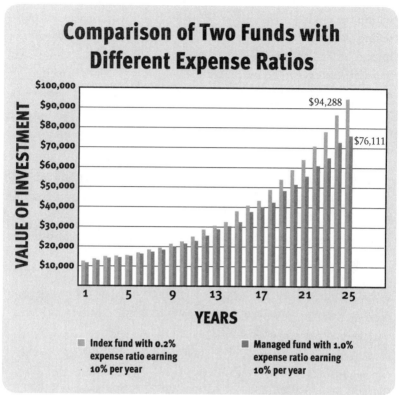

Comparison of Two Funds with Different Expense Ratios

VALUE OF INVESTMENT

$100,000
$90,000 — $94,288
$80,000
$70,000 — $76,111
$60,000
$50,000
$40,000
$30,000
$20,000
$10,000

YEARS
1   5   9   13   17   21   25

■ Index fund with 0.2% expense ratio earning 10% per year

■ Managed fund with 1.0% expense ratio earning 10% per year

FIGURE 8.4

Recognize that index funds, although offering this tremendous tax advantage on a year-by-year basis, are also ticking time bombs. Over a period of time, successful index funds, unlike ETFs, tend to build up a larger amount of embedded gains, and when you buy into the fund you are buying into that existing tax position. If, for example, you decide to invest $10,000 in the Vanguard Index 500, you own a piece of all the stocks currently in that mutual fund. Your share of some of the stocks owned by the fund already is at a profit, since they were bought by the fund over the past 10 or 20 years. For example, those stocks, on average, may have a cost basis of only $4,500, leaving the potential for embedded capital gains of $5,500.

If the market drops precipitously and investors bail out and start selling their shares, the fund manager may be forced to sell shares within the mutual fund to meet the redemption requirements of those selling. As a result, many stocks that are at a substantial gain may need to be sold, and the profit generated on those stocks will be attributed to the investors who do not sell. Thus, with index funds as well as managed funds, during market downturns the value of your mutual fund may drop in value and you could still be stuck with paying taxes on gains realized inside the fund!

> **Today there are easily over a thousand index funds and ETFs (exchange-traded funds) to choose from.**

For example, in the late 1990s, small cap stocks dropped and owners of small cap indexes saw the value of their small cap index funds drop 10% to 15% by the end of the year. Imagine their surprise to find that they were nonetheless being taxed on capital gains equaling 20% of their portfolio! Thus in the example above, if the Vanguard Index were forced to liquidate its holding, you might owe taxes on $2,000 in capital gains, which would cost you about $400 in state and federal capital gains tax.

As index funds have become more popular, they have multiplied exponentially. Today there are easily over a thousand index funds and ETFs to choose from. From the vantage point of a do-it-yourself investor, it is as difficult today to identify the best mix of index funds as it is to select from the myriad of managed equity mutual funds available.

Nonetheless, for small investors, index mutual funds are the best vehicles for investing in large cap stocks. For wealthier investors, it is more tax-efficient to utilize a portfolio of individual stocks. For my clients who have portfolios of more than $1 million, I have developed the Cambridge Index Strategy™, which buys and holds 50 stocks. These stocks, which are owned individually in a portfolio, replicate the three major large cap indexes: Dow Jones, NASDAQ, and the S&P 500. The advantage offered is that losses on individual stocks can be taken short term as deductible capital losses. Long-term gains can be gifted tax free to charities or donor-advised foundations. Often, I advise clients to pay college bills by gifting stocks with a gain to their children to sell. Currently any individual can gift any other person

$12,000 a year (this amount is increased from time to time by Congress) without triggering a gift tax. So let's say a couple gives stock worth $24,000 to a child attending college. The child takes the parents' basis, which means that, for tax purposes, the cost of the stock for the child is the same as it was for his parents. The gain is taxed at the child's bracket, which is much lower than the parents', usually close to zero. The net result is a portfolio where the after-tax return is actually higher than the pretax return. Basically the same result can be obtained with 50 or more large cap stocks in a balanced portfolio.

Small Cap and International Stocks

These equities, unlike large cap stocks, include tens of thousands of little companies. Their information, such as earnings, revenue growth, market share, or productivity, is not well known (some is not even disclosed), and relatively few people study the information available. Their shares tend to be traded in small lots, so even large mutual funds can't get into the market for these shares without impacting the price. As a result, an astute money manager can take advantage of a lot of inefficiencies in this market. Morningstar's research tends to corroborate this finding in that over any 5- or 10-year period, 60% of money managers were able to outperform the market in small cap and international stocks. Again, this figure varies from year to year, from a low of 40% to a high of 60%, but the indication is clear that value can be added by careful selection.

Of course, the fact that the international and small cap indexes do in fact beat 40% of the managers indicates that not every manager is equal. If you are going to rely on fund managers, you must select them carefully and monitor their performance. I am not an advocate of jumping from one manager to the next because performance is less than expected for one or two quarters. Not only does this create a lot of undesirable tax consequences, but it also greatly increases your chances of being whipsawed. (You are whipsawed when you sell one investment that is lousy and buy another with better performance. Then your new investment drops and the original investment turns around and goes up. If you buy back the original, it drops and the one you just sold increases. I hate it when that happens.)

> Generally speaking, I look for reasons why I should not change mutual funds or managers, and when I do, I only change for specific reasons. These include the following:
>
> - Style shift (a small cap fund becomes a large cap fund)
>
> - Management changes in the fund (because, presumably, the manager was the reason that fund was selected in the first place)
>
> - Consistent underperformance over several quarters when compared to funds or managers with the same objective

Over the years, I have found that the managers underperforming the indexes always seem to have good excuses as to why they are not performing as well. Their excuses tend to run the gamut, using terms like *value-picker* or *growth market* or *risk-adjusted return*. The fact is that when you are looking over a 5-year period, these are nothing more than excuses.

Because the volatility of small cap and international investments requires a long-term horizon, they are excellent choices for Roth IRA accounts. This is particularly true because, if actively managed (as they should be), these investments are not very tax-efficient. Holding these investments in a Roth IRA enables the investor with a long investment horizon to maximize the value of tax-free compounded growth. At the same time, the fund manager can buy and sell as needed, and there is no tax impact now or in the future.

International stocks, certain international mutual funds, and gold bullion allow you to hedge the dollar. Many international and global funds use currency hedges to protect their investments against changes in the value of the U.S. dollar. Otherwise, when a Japanese stock that is purchased with yen appreciates, if the dollar strengthens against the yen, the investment could show a loss when converted back to U.S. currency.

I prefer international mutual funds that purposely do not have currency hedges. I believe this is an important function because it protects a portfolio against a weak dollar if we experience higher inflation than other countries. The only way to determine if an international fund uses leverage is to review a mutual fund's portfolio, or call the manager and ask.

Gold also provides this functional protection. For example, gold increased in price from $280 per ounce to over $600 per ounce during this decade. However, gold only increased in U.S. dollars during that period because the dollar weakened. If gold were purchased and sold using euros or yen during the same period, the investment would have lost money in those currencies.

When devising the portfolio allocation of equity investments, we look first to develop a core portfolio of large cap index funds and then balance that with small cap and international funds. Some clients like to give their portfolios a tilt by selecting sector funds, such as technology, health, or biotech.

Specific percentages vary based on the stage of the life cycle and the client's endogenous risk tolerance factors, but the basic guidelines are given here:

- 40% to 60% invested in domestic large cap mutual funds
- 10% to 30% invested in small cap mutual funds
- 20% to 40% invested in foreign mutual funds

Note that today there are an increasing number of fund managers, such as Utopia Funds, who seek to achieve maximum "absolute total return." That means they may buy bonds, large cap stock, international bonds, small cap stocks, and use very sophisticated techniques, such as borrowing on margin, selling short, and other methods. They do not compete against any particular index, but simply buy whatever securities are underpriced, irrespective of what kind of securities they are. Since the asset allocation in these types of funds often shifts dramatically from bonds to cash to large cap funds to international bonds to small cap stocks, an investor does not have the protection of a balanced portfolio. We use mutual funds and separately managed accounts with this orientation primarily in smaller accounts where there is a long investment horizon, such as children's Roth IRAs.

> **If you are going to rely on fund managers, you must select them carefully and monitor their performance.**

Another question that often arises is whether to use separately managed accounts for equities or to use mutual funds. Larger investors are usually better off using separately managed accounts. This is especially true for nonqualified (i.e., after-tax) equity investments. As mentioned earlier, separately managed accounts allow the investor to own the actual shares so it is easier to take advantage of tax benefits. Separate account management also enables investors to customize their holdings (for example, to exclude tobacco stocks if they feel ethically compelled to do so). Management expenses can be somewhat lower with separate accounts than with mutual funds, particularly when large sums (over $500,000) are involved.

Separate accounts have some disadvantages, however. There are high minimums, usually $100,000 to $250,000, as compared to $1,000 or so for mutual funds. This precludes most small investors from using them. More paperwork is also involved, and it is more difficult to switch from one manager to another than it is to sell one mutual fund and buy another.

We also look for the best vehicles to use for these investments. Whenever possible, nonqualified (after-tax) funds are used for large cap equities and Roth IRA (or quasi-Roth) money is used for small cap and international equities. Everyone likes the idea of a portfolio that actually goes up every year instead of going down in some years. Remember: The reality of a well-balanced portfolio using the principles of modern portfolio theory is that there will always be some investments going down in your portfolio while others are increasing in value. It is designed to work that way. Having a balance enables the investor to achieve a higher long-term return while reducing volatility and risk.

We frequently recommend dollar cost averaging (DCA) to clients who are putting new money into the market. This is considered the best alternative to attempting to time the market, the most frequent mistake amateur investors make when trying to find a shortcut to riches. Dollar cost averaging is an investment strategy to avoid putting a large sum of money in the stock market all at one time. Doing so would put all of the investment at risk if the market were to fall drastically. Instead, the amount is invested over 6 months or a year. Then, if the market drops, more shares are bought each month as the market drops. The average cost is whatever the market average is for the period of time investments were averaged. This is a very conservative way to invest new money in the market.

> **Dollar cost averaging is an investment strategy to avoid putting a large sum of money in the stock market all at one time.**

Behavioral finance has demonstrated statistically the futility of market timing. Interestingly, it has also shown that those investors who check their investments more often, and who trade more often, end up with lower investment returns than those who review their portfolio quarterly or annually and rebalance based on endogenous events (ones that occur in their own lives). This is where we see a real-life example of the effects of dysfunctional investor behavior. Most studies now show that it is individual behavior, or dysfunction, that is responsible for most of the losses in any individual's portfolio.

If you are convinced that there is no shortcut, no magic formula, no guru who would enable you to time the market, then you will see the wisdom of diversifying your assets in accordance with modern portfolio theory. Functional Asset Allocation is congruent with modern portfolio theory, but tailors it for the individual investor. Having a functional approach is critical because families are impacted more by endogenous changes in their own lives than by exogenous changes in the economy. The portfolio of the average household is much more complex than that of the institutional investment world. Families need homes and must pay taxes. They have goals other than making the most money possible in the shortest time. Death, divorce, disability, disease, and employment displacement are realities that require a much more variable investment horizon than pension funds and foundations must deal with.

Understanding and utilizing this approach will help you to overcome the particular financial dysfunctions that have impeded your progress in the past and will give you peace of mind on the road to financial freedom.

> "The portfolio of the average houshold is much more complex than that of the institutional investment world."

Now It's Up to You

> ❝You'll never be younger than you are right now.❞
> —BERT WHITEHEAD

In my years as a financial advisor, I have seen all kinds of people, in all circumstances, in all stages of life. I have seen every financial dysfunction you can think of and many you would not imagine—most fixable, some not.

I think I know how doctors feel when they examine people who have been smoking for years, overeating, and living under constant stress. They have neither time for exercise nor time to step back and size up their situation. A physician may feel impatient when such a person comes into the office complaining of ill health. Often the patient doesn't know how to change his habits. Health complexities are too difficult to understand for some people; they may not know where to start.

Making a change can be very frightening, yet at some point, we realize that we must try something different. The truth is that all of us have the ability to make time for what's important to us. But not all of us understand that if we made time for our health, or our wealth, we could enjoy huge benefits in other areas of our lives. The good physical and financial health would ripple into everything else we do, making the things we choose to spend time on happier, better, more successful, more fulfilling. A commitment to better financial fitness is a commitment to everything else in your life. It means financial freedom and the benefits that accompany that freedom.

By reading this book, you have started on the way to changing your financial future. The first step is to understand and accept that the dysfunction you now recognize in yourself is the root of the problem. All of us have some degree of financial dysfunction, but it is difficult to deal with your financial issues until you recognize the source of the problem.

Some dysfunction is caused by misinformation. Inappropriate belief systems handed down through our families are a factor. Our own peculiar personality features may contribute to our dysfunction. Unfortunately, the people we have been told to rely on for financial guidance may be shills, molding solutions to enhance their own financial future. Finally, the financial media feeds this distorted vision of financial success by continually emphasizing short-term solutions.

The key to changing your financial future is to change your exogenously driven paradigm to the sanity of an endogenous approach. No wizard or guru alive can foretell the future of our economy. It is up to you to accept an approach that protects your own future and nurtures your own prosperity.

I hope this book has corrected some of the misinformation you may have had. I hope it has made you realize that the precepts gleaned from your parents regarding money are not necessarily applicable today. The farmers at the turn of the century could not possibly have prepared their children for the blossoming industrial age of the 1920s. The children of Depression and wartime parents could not use their parents' experience to prosper in the 1950s and 1960s. And my generation for the most part has had to learn the new financial realities of the computer age from our children!

> **Making a change can be very frightening, yet at some point, we realize that we must try something different.**

I hope you will realize that media mavens exploit financial ignorance by trying to create critical news events that in fact are irrelevant to the average person. Their posturing as experts may have misled you, by creating the impression that knowing the latest financial fad will make you rich. They play into the hands of their advertisers, who profit from viewers' and listeners' naiveté.

I hope you will distrust any financial advice shaped by a hidden agenda, secret expectations, or ulterior motives. That describes virtually all the advice we get from financial institutions, such as banks, stockbrokers, insurance companies, and mutual fund companies. Not that these institutions don't have a place in our financial lives; indeed, they play a crucial role in helping us implement our plans. We could not have as prosperous a society as we do without them. However, their advice is based on what is good for them, not necessarily what is good for us. Financial advisors whose compensation is based on the outcome of transactions they are advising you about, and who neither recognize nor disclose their obvious conflict of interest, are charlatans. Instead, it is possible to enlist the aid of fee-only fiduciary advisors who as fiduciaries put your interests ahead of their own (see Appendix A).

I hope this book sparks an interest in some of you to decide to become true financial counselors, rather than salespeople for financial products. Perhaps I have offended some sales producers in the financial industry who are ethical and try to do the best for their clients. I hope you are offended because you should expect more of yourself. I hope this book will open your eyes to a higher calling and you will be prompted to leave the dark side of this industry. I urge you to get the credentials you need and decide to work to achieve the goals of your client in a fiduciary capacity rather than selling products or gathering assets to meet the quota of your employer. For some advice on becoming a true fee-only personal financial advisor, see Appendix B.

Alas, unless you are a professional in my field, there are many things to learn, understand, and track in order to achieve and maintain your financial freedom. The subject is a dry one, and it's made as complicated as Congress and vested financial interests can make it. Even though I try to simplify the decisions for my clients and reduce the confusion in their financial lives, I find it is impossible to do away completely with the complexity.

And so all I can tell you is the key ideas I have learned in 35 years that work for real people, written as clearly and simply as I can. I hope you will read this book over several sittings and keep it as a reference for the future.

In addition, I can tell you one more thing. My experience tells me that you can enjoy financial freedom beyond what you think you can, in less time than you believe it will take. We have created for ourselves a daunting financial environment, but it seems to me that the worst part is that simple things are made to seem complex and things requiring only a little time and attention are made to seem overwhelming. I regret that sometimes this misinformation is spread or at least encouraged by people in my own profession, but it is also everywhere around us—a malady of our age.

> You can enjoy financial freedom beyond what you think you can, in less time than you believe it will take.

Many people are able to achieve their financial goals by doing it themselves, just as some people build their own houses. Others will need occasional validation. Many people want financial coaching to help them build the kind of lives they want. Frankly, I do not do my own financial planning. I don't have the objectivity necessary to do my own work. I believe this is the mark of a professional: to acknowledge the need for another perspective.

Unfortunately, not nearly enough true fee-only fiduciary advisors are available to serve the potential market. I have provided some tips and sources for finding and evaluating a fee-only financial planner in Appendix A. In the meantime, I hope this book has helped to fill the gap.

In my practice as a financial advisor, I find that the most powerful solution is encouragement. The second most powerful solution is the willingness to nag my clients when necessary to take simple actions that will benefit them powerfully in their lives.

So let me give you a little bit of encouragement and a little bit of nagging. If you follow some of the simple ideas in this book, with a little bit of diligence, you will put yourself in the top 5% of all people in terms of financial fitness and freedom. If you think that is a worthwhile goal, please put this book in a place where you will see it at least once a week, and try to take a minute to open it up again at least once a month.

In addition, if, after some period your financial fitness starts to improve, don't take that as a sign that you should neglect it. Continue on the same path, spending a little time here and there to maintain your progress, until, like jogging and eating right, it becomes a habit.

And if all of this works for you, then give a copy of this book as a gift to a friend who is struggling with financial dysfunctions, trying to achieve financial freedom. With all the misinformation swirling around us, it might never find its way to your friend otherwise.

As I said in Chapter 1, I hope this book helps achieve more financial freedom for middle-income Americans. Having read this book, financial freedom is within your grasp. It's up to you to make it happen.

Where to Find a True Fee-Only Personal Financial Advisor/Fiduciary

Once people realize that fee-only fiduciary advisors are available, they usually want to find one for themselves. The good news is that the number of fee-only planners is growing much faster than the rest of the industry. In 1990 only 5% of all people who said they did financial planning identified themselves as "fee only." Fifteen years later, nearly 40% did.

The bad news is that true fee-only advisors are still very scarce; many of those who call themselves "fee only" are not actually fiduciary advisors. Because the fee-only approach has become so popular, many commissioned salespeople, like those at American Express, have started calling themselves "fee based" or "fee and commission." That means they charge you a small fee (under $1,000 usually) and run all your information through their computer, which prints out what they call a financial plan.

At that point, you discover that to secure your financial future you have to buy their proprietary mutual funds (which ensures that the salesperson makes the most money he can, possibly more than you will). Oh, you will also need to buy a whole bunch of their life insurance, and only permanent will do (which is again where the salespeople make the most money). If you are elderly or obviously naive, you will definitely need some annuities, which are sold to their most financially vulnerable customers. Annuities also happen to pay out even higher commissions than mutual funds.

Some salespeople have the audacity to claim they do both fee-only planning and commission-based planning. Trust me on this: They make a whole lot more money on commissions than on flat fees. Somehow, you will end up with commissioned products because they don't want to "leave any money on the table."

A recent rule promulgated by the SEC requires all those calling themselves "financial planners" to take fiduciary responsibility in working with clients. This would seem to draw a bright line between sales reps and fee-only financial advisors, but purveyors of financial products have found a way around it. Now if you go to a sales rep for one of these companies that purport to do "financial planning," the sales rep has you fill out a form that is sent to a Certified Financial Planner at a separate company owned by the wirehouse. The CFP there is the one who presumably has a fiduciary obligation to you, even though you never meet her.

Often the way that compensation is structured is a clue to whether the planner is a fee-only fiduciary advisor. If the advisor charges an hourly rate or a fixed annual retainer, then he is likely a fee-only fiduciary advisor. If it turns out that you are paying commissions, then the advisor is a sales rep.

Since the 1990s there has been a huge shift to charging customers a percentage of assets under management, usually 1.5% to 2.0% per year, with a sliding scale used for assets in excess of $1 million. The problem with this arrangement is that you can't tell whether the advisor is merely a sales rep, or if she is a fee-only fiduciary advisor. Both may be considered "fee only," but they may or may not be fiduciaries. This is not clean enough to suit me, but it is a marked improvement over transaction-based commissions. These sales reps are called *asset gatherers*, which isn't a compliment, as I explain later. The asset management fee is supposed to cover all transaction costs so the broker has no incentive to churn accounts (that is, to continually buy and sell). Incredibly, some brokers who have shifted to this approach charge commissions *in addition* to their asset management slice.

Here's a secret you need to know if you have now hired or are thinking of hiring an asset gatherer. They are paid based on how many assets they can gather up to be managed by their company. There is intense competition now because all the brokers are getting into this game. Therefore, the fees quoted are highly negotiable. You should not be paying more than 1.0% (or 100 basis points) for this service if it involves domestic equities, and a lot less if you are a high-net-worth client.

> " Asset gatherers have built-in conflicts of interest because it is in their best interest to have control over as much money as possible.

Harold Evensky, in his book *Wealth Management*, identifies three types of advisors (excluding salespeople): money managers, asset gatherers, and wealth managers. I agree with his classifications.

Money managers are the people actually involved in analyzing various stocks and deciding which ones to buy. The best of these, generally but not always, are running large mutual funds. You can't expect to have a personal relationship with them; usually they won't even talk to you unless you have an 8-figure portfolio.

Asset gatherers are essentially salespeople who like to talk a lot about asset allocation. That is important, but it's only a small part of your financial life. Because they are paid based on the amount of assets gathered, obviously that is what they are most interested in. Some make a show of doing comprehensive financial planning, but it is usually incidental to their main job: gathering more assets.

Asset gatherers have built-in conflicts of interest because it is in their best interest to have control over as much money as possible. If you want advice on whether to pay off the mortgage on your house, roll over your IRA, gift money to your children, or set up a donor-advised foundation, you can't expect unbiased advice from asset gatherers. In these and many other situations, their compensation is impacted by the outcome of the transaction. For example, consider a client who is leaving a job and wondering if she should move her

401(k) to her new employer, leave it where it is, or roll it over into an IRA that the advisor manages. Since these pensions can represent a significant portion of a client's assets as well as a large sum of money, there is potential for a huge conflict of interest. In my opinion, mere disclosure is not adequate for a fiduciary in such circumstances; rather, the advisor must recuse himself. This means he should explain the conflict to the client and require her to go get an independent, disinterested opinion from another financial advisor. Both the recusal and the independent opinion should be confirmed in writing.

I have seen reprehensible abuses when asset gatherers charge a low fee (e.g., 0.50% to 0.75%) for managing cash and bonds and a higher fee (1.5% to 2.0%) on equities. I have worked with clients who have come to me from advisors using this approach, and it is apparent that the advisors tilt the portfolio heavily toward equities, since they make three times as much for "managing" these securities. One client who came to me had 97% of his assets in stocks—and he was only 3 months from retirement! Even an aggressive allocation in that situation would not justify investing more than 60% in stocks.

Note that asset gatherers don't actually manage your investments, other than occasionally to review your asset allocation. They either put you in mutual funds or hire a money manager (if you have investments in the 6 figures) with whom they split the fee. In my opinion, these people are parasites. They really add little if any value because they only focus on the assets they manage. They don't know very much about real estate or taxes. Often they will sell you an insurance policy if they can.

There is also a danger when working with advisors who charge a percentage of assets under management that they will focus only on your investments and not address the other aspects of your financial life, such as estate planning, tax planning, or goal setting. After all, people usually do what they are paid to do, and if they are paid to manage assets, that's all you'll get for the most part.

I can never understand how these advisors get away with charging the same percentage every year. Most of the work with a client is done the first year, so it seems reasonable for the fee to drop in later years.

Of course, when the market drops a few years in a row, their fees drop as well, so then it is not a great business to be in.

Even the asset gatherers who only charge 1% of assets under management are grossly overpaid for what they do. On a portfolio of $500,000, their continuing fee is $5,000. The first year there is some value added perhaps in restructuring a portfolio that could justify the fee, but in succeeding years, they generally spend only 2 to 3 hours with a client and 1 to 2 hours reviewing the portfolio, since all their portfolios are structured in aggregate. I think this failure to add value on a continuing basis will impact their survival in the next 5 years.

Recently, asset gatherers have been under a lot of pressure because they are being commoditized as increasingly they are required to compete on price alone. Commissioned salespeople are deciding that they would rather be asset managers because it doesn't require any more education. So competition is driving down fees. During the first part of this decade we were in a bear market. Their assets dwindled so their income dropped. Finally, their clients are leaving in droves because they can't seem to understand why they should pay $10,000 or $20,000 a year to someone to lose money for them.

These factors have hurt revenues of many asset management firms. Drops of 25% to 40% per year in their revenue are not uncommon, due to falling asset bases, client desertion, and more competition. The gravy train is coming to an end.

Wealth managers are true financial advisors, and the best are comprehensive, fee-only, personal financial advisors who work in a fiduciary relationship with their clients. They take a holistic approach and incorporate tax planning, if not tax preparation, as well as estate planning and regular updates on all your investments. They review insurance needs regularly and keep clients focused on their financial goals. They also monitor your investments across the board to maintain appropriate asset allocation. Although they usually do utilize money managers, they do not receive compensation from them. They are paid to be your agent and make sure you get the best deal.

Beware of labels. There is no truth in advertising in this industry. Insurance salespeople call themselves wealth managers, commissioned mutual fund salespeople call themselves financial planners, and stockbrokers call themselves investment bankers. Therefore, you have to look deeper and find out how these people actually work and where exactly they earn their money.

The very worst prospective advisors will try to sidestep your question about how much they earn from your investments. They ask, "If this is a good investment for you, what difference does it make how much I earn?" This is a clue: This person thinks you are a chump and will rip you off. Get away fast.

How your financial planner is compensated critically determines what advice you will get. It is the key difference between an advisor and a salesperson. Salespeople only need to know a script and how to manipulate their customers' emotions. Salespeople don't have to create value, or the value creation is incidental; all they have to do is close the sale.

Thus, hiding fees is very important, and advisors who are salespeople often make huge amounts of money. If advisors are compensated either on a flat rate, an hourly rate, or on some formula that is understandable, they can only survive if their advice creates enough value for the client to justify their employment.

How a person is compensated also determines in what areas she is most knowledgeable. If a fee-and-commission advisor sells commissionable insurance policies, that is where she will make the most money. Most likely, she will not know very much about other investment choices, like U.S. savings bonds. Likewise, a Merrill Lynch asset gatherer will probably not know a lot about no-load mutual funds or the financial intricacies of buying a home. Many fee-only advisors' knowledge of commissioned products may be more limited than that of the salespeople who are hired to sell those products. But fee-only advisors are geared to truly comprehensive planning, and they are more knowledgeable than salespeople with the same amount of experience.

It amazes me how people who are otherwise very frugal often don't know how much the financial advice they are getting really costs them. Our industry's most financially successful players are masters of concealment. They like to hide your fees in a brokerage statement or in a prospectus in tiny print so you won't notice them. Do yourself a favor and find out now how much your advisor is costing you.

HOW TO EVALUATE A PERSONAL FINANCIAL ADVISOR

Once you have sorted out the salespeople from the real advisors, you must evaluate them. The place to start is with their credentials. Look for credentials offered by credible educational and professional institutions, such as an MBA, CPA, or JD. The other designation I respect is the EA (enrolled agent), who is licensed to practice before the IRS. These degrees or designations, however, don't necessarily indicate that the advisor is knowledgeable about financial planning, but they are a good start.

Without a doubt, the standard of the financial planning industry has become the CFP (certified financial planner) designation. Although I don't have a CFP, I consider it to be a critical requirement for the advisors who work with my clients. This designation is trademarked and ensures a well-rounded knowledge of the various areas of financial planning. It requires increasingly rigorous preparation, as well as ongoing education to maintain the credential.

> Without a doubt, the standard of the financial planning industry has become the CFP (certified financial planner) designation.

I am sometimes asked why I am not a CFP because I believe so strongly in it. I started as a financial planner many years before the CFP was available. I have never felt I needed it to bolster recognition of my competence. I still support it, however, because such a designation, as it tightens its requirements, is critical if financial planning is to develop into a true profession.

There are other credentials as well, such as PFS, CLU, CFA, ChFC, and so on. If you interview someone with one of these acronyms after his name, you can find out how he thinks his designation enhances his advice. In fact, many of these other credentials are very industry specific. Too often, they are promulgated by segments of our industry that have a vested interest in making their salespeople appear qualified. I suggest giving preference to the mainstream designations just reviewed.

Also, evaluate a prospective advisor's prior experience in depth. The time she spent working for a bank, an insurance company, or as a stockbroker is related but not necessarily relevant. Focus on the experience she has had as a personal financial advisor. Find out the demographic profile of the other clients she works with to see if their backgrounds are similar to yours in terms of income, net worth, age, goals, and occupation.

I believe it is very important to ask for at least three references of clients whose circumstances and goals are similar to yours. If the advisor refuses to give referrals, using the excuse that it violates confidentiality, just walk away. If you get references, obviously these are people who are expected to give you positive feedback. That means you should take heed of anything negative.

Call the clients and ask specific as well as open-ended questions:

- Is the advisor prompt in returning phone calls?
- Are the appointments focused, or does she ramble?
- Does the advisor complete assignments on time?
- What do you consider to be her strongest area of expertise?
- What is her weakest area?
- How long have you worked together?
- What would be your biggest reservation in referring her to friends?

Advisors who are properly credentialed but just starting out can still be very good candidates if they are bright, ethical, and upfront about their experience. Advisors with newer practices generally keep abreast of more recent developments in financial planning, they are more computer literate if they were born after 1965, and they will have more time to work with you. They also generally charge less than experienced advisors with established practices. Younger advisors are more likely to outlive you, and you may have the pleasure later on of being one of their clients with high seniority, which every advisor cherishes.

It is a good sign if more experienced advisors have a training program to bring along the next generation of fee-only advisors. I think teaching the next generation is not only a professional mandate but the best way to keep current and up-to-date. An established firm with no progression path for new advisors generally doesn't have an adequate succession plan in place.

Be sure to ask the advisor to give you a copy of his "Form ADV," which every advisor is required to register with the SEC or the state in order to be a registered investment advisor (RIA). An RIA is required by law to provide this document, either in brochure form or as a copy of the one filed. Ask for a copy of the one filed and read through it carefully. Although the form is as obnoxious as a government form can be, it is easier to read each successive time. The ADV will let you know if the RIA has ever declared bankruptcy or has had any complaints filed against him or criminal convictions. It should also explain the fee schedule, so you can see if it conforms to what you have been told.

If an advisor is not an RIA or cannot provide you with a copy of the ADV filed, forget it. The advisor is probably a salesperson and has a broker-dealer who is registered with the National Association of Security Dealers (NASD). Insurance agents only need a state-issued Series 7 license, so they seldom have RIAs. Even if an agent has a CFP and is an RIA, he may not be a fee-only fiduciary advisor; the easiest way to find out is to ask him point blank, and then ask him to point it out in his ADV.

Also, find out what professional organizations the advisor belongs to and how active she is. Active membership in professional organizations is usually a good measure of how current the advisor is and if she is diligent about acquiring continuing education. Errors and omissions insurance is generally available through these organizations. Find out if the advisor you are considering has that coverage in the event that a mistake is made.

Here are some additional badges of competence:

- Does the advisor use cold calls, advertisements (other than directory listings), or hold seminars to try to attract new clients? The best advisors do not have to resort to direct marketing; rather, they depend on referrals from their current clients for new clients. This is a very good sign.

- Does the advisor receive fees or fee splits from any other source? If you are not paying your fee directly, and if compensation is not limited to the fees paid directly, this is a clue that the advisor may not be a true fee-only advisor. You may want to ignore occasional consulting fees, fees for expert testimony, writing income, and so on, because those activities are not likely to conflict with your interests. However, if fees are received from other sources, including referral fees, that could indicate a conflict of interest. A captive advisor who is a pawn of Schwab or another organization and paid by that company (even if it comes out of your account) or who is required to split fees with that firm is not truly your agent.

- Does the prospective advisor have someone else review his own personal financial plan? A badge of true professionals is that they don't practice their profession on themselves. Doctors don't take out their own appendixes; lawyers shouldn't represent themselves; therapists don't counsel themselves. Keep in mind that, to a large extent, advisors suggest investments they hold themselves. So if they are missing something in their portfolio, you will likely end up with the same problem. I have always had my own personal financial advisor because it is too difficult for me to be objective about my own situation. I can easily be detached when I work with you, but my own affairs are laden with my personal anxieties and dysfunctions. Worse yet, my own planning won't get done.

Granted, only a top few planners meet all these criteria, so you will have to be flexible. Nevertheless, each criterion has a function, so you should be aware of the danger you are assuming if your chosen advisor falls short.

The advisor will also want to be evaluating you as a prospective client. Bring in a list of assets and liabilities as well as tax returns (if requested) to be reviewed. Ideally, you will want to get a sample of the advice you would be getting. It doesn't make any sense to pay a sizable sum of money to an advisor who is going to tell you to do things you don't want to do. Nor does it make sense to hire one to tell you to keep on doing what you are already doing. Ask for some examples of advice the advisor would be giving you that is different from what you have been doing. Ask for an explanation of the reasons for whatever she's suggesting. Then evaluate the answer to see if you can understand it and if it makes any sense to you.

WHERE TO START LOOKING

Here is a short list of the organizations I think are credible. I have also summarized my thoughtful consideration of their advantages and disadvantages. The organizations are listed in order of the ones I consider best to those that are least preferable.

The Alliance of Cambridge Advisors

The Alliance of Cambridge Advisors is an alliance of fee-only financial personal advisors committed to serving middle-income people and using a holistic approach. Its advisors charge a flat fee or an annual retainer fee, which usually includes tax preparation and financial planning as well as handling your investments. Naturally, since I founded this group in 1995, I would have to think it is terrific.

Advantages include having the highest standard of professional requirements in the industry. Advisors must be a CFP or equivalent to be trained, as well as a tax background. Most are attorneys, CPAs, or EAs. Advisors with mature practices are required to be full NAPFA members (see below) and subscribe to the highest standard of ethics in the industry. They have a clear progression path to train new advisors.

Although each of the advisors is a separate RIA, they are trained in the Cambridge core concepts outlined in this book. While many advisors have modified these concepts to fit their particular practices, all of them share a common approach, which ensures continuity if you move and have to change advisors.

Cambridge Advisors primarily serve clients on an ongoing basis and charge a fixed annual retainer fee. Most of them also make available "Financial Tune-ups" or "Financial Reviews" to reach a broad market. These are designed for clients who have only two or three financial questions to ask. The charge of these appointments is generally $500 to $1,000 and includes 2 to 4 hours, with no further obligations. The specificity of the advice is inversely proportional to the complexity of the issues raised.

Drawbacks include the relative scarcity of the Alliance's advisors, since at this writing they include only about 135 advisors nationwide. There is also a relatively large range in the experience level of the advisors. The more experienced advisors generally charge higher fees.

For more information and a list of the group's advisors, go to its Web site at www.CambridgeAdvisors.com or call toll free 888-834-6333. New advisors transitioning from commissioned practices are not listed on the Web site until they have stopped receiving commissions from the sale of financial products.

The National Association of Personal Financial Advisors

The National Association of Personal Financial Advisors (NAPFA), founded in 1983, is a professional organization of fee-only fiduciary advisors with about 750 members and affiliates. I have been an active member of NAPFA for nearly 20 years. Advisors who meet its standards are referred to as "NAPFA-registered financial advisors." They must meet rigorous entrance requirements, including a peer review of a financial plan they have prepared. They are also required to meet very intense and broad continuing education requirements. Their objective is "to provide consumers and institutions with comprehensive and objective financial advice on a 'fee-only' basis, keeping only the best interests of the client in mind—with neither the advisor nor any related party receiving compensation contingent on the purchase or sale of a financial product."

The role of NAPFA-registered financial advisors is defined to include the three C's of financial planning:	• *Comprehensive* planning that takes into consideration all of a client's needs and goals, and is regularly reviewed and updated • The highest standards of *Competence* • *Compensation* untainted by any type of fee received by the vendors of financial products, including investment funds, insurance companies, and estate attorneys.

The advantages of using referrals from NAPFA is that they have a wide base of advisors and are definitely recognized as the elite planners in the industry in terms of ethics and commitment to fee-only planning. Even with its relatively small membership, NAPFA has influenced the financial industry significantly. NAPFA-registered financial advisors can be counted on to meet clear recognized standards of competence, which gives you a benchmark to use as a selection criterion. The organization will provide you with an interview form to evaluate financial advisors.

NAPFA's members do not all share a common approach, which is a drawback. Many of its members have developed into pure asset gatherers; while technically they are supposed to offer comprehensive planning, often this service is not provided. Most do not prepare personal income tax returns as part of their comprehensive services. Many of the NAPFA-registered financial advisors have small boutique practices catering to the very wealthy or are closed to new clients. The experience level of the advisors is quite varied. In addition, the consumer is not allowed to access a list of advisors online. You must submit a request on the group's site and then representatives will mail or e-mail you a list.

More information about NAPFA can be obtained, and referrals can be requested, on its Web site at www.NAPFA.org or by calling toll free 800-366-2732.

Garrett Financial Network

Garrett Financial Network (GFN) is a network of fee-only financial planners who serve the broad consumer market using a doctor's office model: Clients can hire a GFN advisor on an hourly basis, generally $100 to 150 per hour. Sheryl Garrett, who has been a board member of NAPFA, founded the network in 2000. The network has listed over two hundred affiliated advisors. GFN training is primarily geared to administrative issues relating to using the network's business format, rather than a particular theoretical approach. The availability of fee-only hourly advice for middle-income people is very much needed. It is not clear how GFN screens its advisors on an ongoing basis to make sure they are truly fee only rather than fee based.

Advantages include accessibility, especially for do-it-yourselfers who just want general advice on their financial situation. A substantial number of the network advisors are relatively inexperienced, so their fees tend to be lower. The Web site does have a handy list of advisors by region.

Some of the drawbacks include an apparent lack of minimum credentials, so there is a wide variability in the competence of people in the network. Most of GFN's advisors do not prepare tax returns or give tax advice on any complex issues. A few network advisors are members of NAPFA, but that affiliation is not required. Billing hourly does not lend itself to comprehensive planning; ongoing retainers are based on an asset-gathering model. The most successful advisors in GFN generally gravitate to building an asset-gathering practice.

You can get more information about Garrett Financial Network by calling toll free 866-260-8400 or by visiting its Web site, http://www.garrettplanningnetwork.com.

Financial Planning Association

The Financial Planning Association (FPA) is the largest association of financial planners in the country, with a membership of over 10,000. It has become the so-called official organization for CFPs, although members who joined earlier than 1999 have been grandfathered in. I am a member of this organization.

FPA has a referral program for prospective clients, although members must opt in. That is good because members who have closed practices are not listed. It is bad because some of the best practices choose not to be listed because they are bothered with too many unqualified inquiries.

Its primary advantage is its size, covering every state in the union, all 25 Standard Metropolitan Statistical Areas (SMSAs), and most other cities and towns with populations over 100,000. In addition, all the members listed are required to have CFPs, so you get a well-screened list.

The disadvantage is that well over half the planners listed are salespeople working for brokerage houses, insurance companies, or commissioned financial planning firms. Most of the remainder are asset gatherers.

The number of fee-only advisors in the FPA has grown considerably. It also has an excellent educational program, many parts of which are available to the public. You can get more information from its Web site at http://www.fpanet.org or by calling 800-322-4237.

How to Become a True Fee-Only Personal Financial Advisor

I hope this book will motivate at least some of you to consider a career as a fee-only personal financial advisor. The demand for unbiased advice from all income levels across the country is growing exponentially. I am convinced that the primary limitation to the growth of our profession is the inadequate supply of advisors.

Fee-only advisors today are well compensated on about the same level as other professionals with similar training and experience. Often the pay is low to start, because it costs a firm more to train you in the first 6 to 12 months than you are able to produce.

The most salient reason to consider this career, however, is the tremendous satisfaction derived from really making a positive impact on clients' lives. Studies have shown consistently that fee-only advisors are ranked as one of the five most important people in their clients' lives. There is the advantage of working with the same families year after year. Once established, most of the revenue generated is renewal revenue, and if you structure your practice right, 95% of your clients renew every year.

There are two drawbacks to becoming a fee-only advisor. One is that it takes courage, effort, and time to get a practice started, although this is certainly true of any profession. The second is that this career, even more than most other professions, requires a great deal of continuing education. The half-life of the knowledge in our profession is 18 months! So every 18 months, half of everything you know becomes obsolete.

WHO IS SUITED TO BE A FEE-ONLY ADVISOR?

I have trained people from all types of backgrounds over the past 35 years. I have listed here the qualifications of those who are well suited to this profession in order of the success rate I have seen. I have also noted the next step for those who are not currently suited but who could be with additional education.

Well-suited are advisors employed as salespeople in the financial industry who have come to realize that the more ethical they are, the less money they make. They are uncomfortable with the company line and frequently give advice that is right for the client but not appreciated by their employer. If you have a college degree and a CFP, you are ready to transition.

An old myth still circulates that if you go into fee-only planning you have to starve for 2 or 3 years. We have found that advisors who transition from being sales reps make more income their first year as fee-only advisors than they did the year before on commissions. Your best bet is to affiliate with a fee-only firm or start your own practice. The reason you are very likely to be successful in a short time is that you already have a flow of prospects, and it is relatively easy to convert current clients. If they liked you as a salesperson, they'll love you as a fiduciary advisor!

> **Studies have shown consistently that fee-only advisors are ranked as one of the five most important people in their clients' lives.**

It is worthwhile to check out the programs offered by Cambridge Advisors, NAPFA, and GFN (see Appendix A). They all have training programs for transitioning advisors.

If you are in sales in the financial industry, but don't have a degree or a CFP, your Series 6 or 7 license won't be enough. Start the CFP program now, if possible, to combine with college courses you have previously taken. Finish your degree at the same time you finish the CFP program. It is best to look for a paraplanner job at a fee-only firm in the meantime if you can. If you are determined to begin immediately, you may be accepted by the GFN for its training, but it is difficult to be a successful fee-only planner without credentials.

If you presently have a law practice, a tax practice, or are a CPA, you are in a perfect position to upgrade your practice to be a fee-only advisor. You already have the respect of your clients, and they count on you to be unbiased. Your current clients likely want to get their financial planning advice from you.

To get the right background and set up an efficient system, consider the Personal Financial Services (PFS) designation if you are a CPA; otherwise, go for a CFP. You may well be able to test out of one or more of the six curriculum parts of the CFP training. To integrate this into your current practice, consider the programs listed by Cambridge Advisors, NAPFA, and GFN.

If you are a college-educated professional changing careers, you may well consider a second career as a fee-only financial advisor. You would need to get a CFP, which can be obtained through a correspondence course. New advisors with this background are usually very successful by their own standards, since they generally have another income source. They have time to build their practice to the level they can enjoy. Often they practice out of their home. You will get rolling much more quickly if you take training courses offered by Cambridge Advisors, NAPFA, or GFN.

If you are a young person in college or just graduating from college, I would suggest that you find a paraplanner position to start in the business with a fee-only firm in your area. This will count toward the 3-year internship required to use the CFP designation. Don't be fooled by big-name financial firms that advertise financial planning jobs on campus. They claim they will hire you, train you, and in 6 months, you will be a financial advisor.

What actually will happen is they will pay you a subsistence salary until you pass your Series 7 exam, then put you on commission with a list of phone numbers and you will start dialing for dollars. If you have a snappy line of chatter, a thick enough skin to shrug off a 95% rejection rate, and make enough cold calls, you can earn a lot of money very fast. But don't kid yourself: You didn't become a financial advisor, you became a salesperson.

Check out the NAPFA Web site (www.NAPFA.org), which runs a list of help wanted ads placed by fee-only firms around the country.

> **If you presently have a law practice, a tax practice, or are a CPA, you are in a perfect position to upgrade your practice to be a fee-only advisor.**

If you are a salesperson outside the financial industry or already employed by a firm in the industry, and you enjoy the thrill of the kill in closing sales and moving on to find bigger game, you won't want to become a fee-only planner. As a high producer, you are creating value for your employer because you can prospect effectively, bring in cases, and schmooze with clients. You can make a lot of money fast for the present time, but I think the Death of a Salesman era in the emerging financial profession will soon force you to find something else to sell.

Fee-only planning requires different skills and an ethical standard necessary to establish an ongoing fiduciary relationship as an unbiased advisor to a client, which is incompatible with a sales orientation.

WHAT WILL YOU NEED?

Once you have your credentials, you will need to register as an investment advisor if you intend to have your own practice. Usually this will be with your state or as many states where you will be advising clients. Usually states have a *de minimis* requirement of five clients, so if you have fewer than that, you don't have to register. If you happen to have over $25 million under management, you may be able to register federally with the SEC and avoid state filings.

Some states require you to take a Series 2 or 65 licensing exam before you practice, even if you work with an established firm. These tests are not especially difficult; if you have passed the CFP comprehensive, you will have no problem with this one. Beyond that, not much capital is required to open your own practice. You will need an office, office furniture, a computer (faster is better), and a telephone.

Marketing is the tough part, as well as figuring out how to do financial planning efficiently. All four organizations described in Appendix A have training programs that attendees have found very helpful. It is definitely worthwhile to avail yourself of one of these programs to help get your practice started. You will save many times their cost by avoiding mistakes and learning how to attract clients.

SUGGESTED READING FOR ASPIRING PLANNERS

Nancy Langdon Jones, CFP, *So You Want to Be a Financial Planner* (Advisorpress, 2005). Available through Barnes & Noble.com or through the author's Web site: www.nancysbooks.com.

Mary Rowland, *Best Practices for Financial Advisors* (New York: Bloomberg Press, 1997). Available through Barnes & Noble.com or on Bloomberg's Web site: www.bloomberg.com/books.

About the Author

Bert was born in Bisbee, Arizona. His financial career began as a runner and board boy for the local E.F. Hutton agency when he was 12 years old. His job was to pick up the telegram with daily closing NYSE quotes from Western Union after school and mark them on the huge blackboard on the wall of the stock brokerage office. His boss, P.J. Meenan, had worked there since the turn of the century and taught Bert the fundamentals of investing.

He has a B.A. in psychology, an M.B.A. in finance, and a law degree. He started practicing as a tax attorney and fee-only financial planner, serving primarily executives, professionals, and small business owners, in 1972.

Bert organized Cambridge Connection, Inc. in 1983, using a holistic approach to fee-only tax and financial advisory services. He currently personally advises clients across the country.

In 1995 Bert formed a new organization, Cambridge Advisors, LLC, which has evolved into the Alliance of Cambridge Advisors. LLC., a nonprofit organization. This organization trains new advisors and supports mature firms on a national basis in the Cambridge approach to holistic fee-only financial planning, much of which is outlined in this book. Over 250 advisors have been trained in the Cambridge System™, with classes offered on an ongoing basis.

He is the author of *Why Smart People Do Stupid Things with Money: Overcoming Financial Dysfunction* and nine other books relating to personal finance.

Bert has been selected by *Worth Magazine* as one of the best 100 personal financial advisors in the United States every year since 1994. He is regularly quoted in the *Wall Street Journal*, *Newsweek*, *Money* magazine, *Kiplinger's*, *Forbes*, *The New York Times*, *The Washington Post*, *Investment News*, *Bloomberg*, *U.S. News & World Report*, *Investment Advisor*, and *Detroit News/Free Press*. He has also been a guest on Fox Money Line.

Bert was also featured on P.B.S. television on a two-hour special to be run nationwide in 2007 titled "Why Smart People Do Stupid Things with Money."

Index